Suburban Sahibs

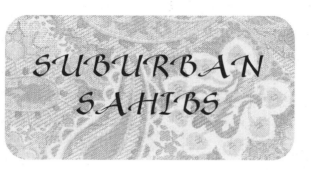

SUBURBAN SAHIBS

Three Immigrant Families

and

Their Passage

from

India to America

S. MITRA KALITA

Rutgers University Press
New Brunswick, New Jersey, and London

Manufactured in the United States of America

Library of Congress Cataloging-in-Publication Data

Kalita, S. Mitra, 1976–
Suburban Sahibs : three immigrant families and their passage from India to America / S. Mitra Kalita.
p. cm.
Includes bibliographical references.
ISBN 0-8135-3318-X (hardcover : alk. paper)
1. East Indian Americans—New Jersey—Middlesex County—Social conditions. 2. East Indian Americans—Cultural assimilation—New Jersey—Middlesex County. 3 East Indian Americans—New Jersey—Middlesex County—Biography. 4. Immigrants—New Jersey—Middlesex County—Social conditions. 5. Immigrants—New Jersey—Middlesex County—Biography. 6. New Jersey—Emigration and immigration—Case studies. 7. India—Emigration and immigration—Case studies. 8. Asian American families—New Jersey—Middlesex County—Case studies. 9. Suburban life—New Jersey—Middlesex County—Case studies. 10. Middlesex County (N.J.)—Ethnic relations. I. Title.
F142.M6K35 2003
929' .2'08991411073—dc21
2003005658

British Cataloging-in-Publication information for this book is available from the British Library.

For Ma and Papa

Contents

Acknowledgments

This book would not have been possible without the Kotharis, the Patels, and the Sarmas. Over the course of three years, Pradip, Nandini, Payal, Toral, Harish, Kapila, Kajal, Zankhana, Sankumani, Shravani, and Chiku let me into their lives, homes, and selves so readily and willingly. May others be as inspired by their stories as I have been.

I thank Samuel Freedman of Columbia University Graduate School of Journalism for showing me how it's done, and for giving me the confidence to do it. I thank him for the words and mantras and rules that echoed in my ears when my typing fingers couldn't go on and then somehow did. I thank my fellow "folks," Jeffrey Goldfarb, David Lawrence, Jana Karam, Harry Bruinius, Shira Boss, Dore Carroll, and Sarah Richards, for their encouragement along the way. I especially thank Dave for helping me navigate uncharted waters, pun intended. And I must single out Jeff, who quoted from *The Crucible* and proved over and over just how much he really cares about books, and me. I thank the entire Book Seminar class of 2000 for their comments, edits, and advice—all of which influenced the pages that follow.

I thank Marlie Wasserman of Rutgers University Press for taking a chance on a fledgling writer, for seeing this as a viable subject, and for her encouragement of my career and endeavors beyond this book. I also thank her assistant and my college classmate Michele Gisbert. I thank copy editor India Cooper for her close reading and patience.

I thank Russell Galen of the Scovil Chichak Galen Literary Agency for helping me navigate the world of book contracts, and agent Anna Ghosh for facilitating our introduction.

I thank Beth Kressel, who served as my research assistant and worked miracles in tracking down information in a short amount of time.

I thank Vikram Tank, who devised and executed the idea for the cover image.

I thank Niraj Kaji, Mukul Pandya, and Maryann Skinner, none of whom know each other but all of whom encouraged me to take the time off to do it right. Mukul's advice, delivered over a Gujarati thali, especially resonated: "You *must* write this book in New Jersey."

Most of this book was completed while I was a reporter for *Newsday*'s New York City edition. For their support, I thank my former colleagues, especially Rich Galant, Vickie Elmer, and Katia Hetter. They rank among the smartest people I know in this business. Bob Keeler showed me an organizational system that, even at a fraction of his obsessive level, still helped tremendously. Ray Sanchez offered regular doses of comfort from having been there, assuring me that *todo* really would be *bien*. Also at *Newsday,* I thank Steve Sink, Curtis Taylor, Mohamad Bazzi, Sumathi Reddy, Mae Cheng, John Mancini, Tony Marro, Laura Mann, Iris Quigley, Fred Bruning, James Madore, Pradnya Joshi, Tom Incantalupo, Howard Schneider, and Charlotte Hall.

I thank my editors at the *Washington Post,* Alison Howard, Scott Vance, Robert Barnes, Jo-Ann Armao, Milton Coleman, Steve Coll, and Leonard Downie.

Navigating India would not have been possible without the help of my family, who are too many to name and all too dear to choose. I single out Aita, my grandmother and one of the wisest souls I know. She will never be able to read these words, but her spirit influenced every one of them. Also in India, I thank the entire Lajmi family, the Captain, Lalitha, and Kalpana; Venkatwareshalu in Bombay; Arindom Goswami and his wife, Anandita, and Kemas Wadia and his family in Baroda; Kaberi Talukdar and the Phukan family in Assam.

I thank my friends Sreenath Sreenivasan and Roopa Unnikrishnan, who offered steady advice and home-cooked meals. Sree, who taught me my earliest lessons in reporting on one's own community, jokingly calls himself my agent; he is so much more: a mentor, friend, role model. I also thank the members of the South Asian Journalists Association who reached out to help and offer sources.

I thank numerous members of the Assamese community of North America who served as my extended family and biggest fans throughout my life.

In addition, I thank, in no particular order, Muffin Lord, Lauren Lineback, Angela Tsai, Sapreet Saluja, Pete Bigelow, Jennifer Frantz, Lori Kagan, Natalie Kuszmerski, Sendhil Revuluri, David Sheehan, Alaudin, Jason Hsiao, Rajesh Paremeswaran, Raj Chand, Siddhartha Chowdhary, Sai Koppola, Stony Grunow, Monica Mehta, and Jyoti Thottam. I thank Thom Powers for his suggestion of the title.

I thank Shaan Akbar, Krishan Patel, and Arnab Datta, who served as my audience and friends during a lonely book leave. I also thank Shivank Gupta, who crooned a perfectly pitched "Beauty School Dropout," forcing me to realize the Indian invasion had even hit Rydell High School.

I thank Suketu Mehta for his characterization of Bombay, Ashok Parameswaran for his expertise on globalization and emerging markets (not to mention an ensuing friendship), and Brian Selander for his steady forwards on articles about Middlesex County politics and additional insights.

Several people reviewed portions of the manuscript, and I specifically thank Melanie Cooper-Cortese, Sapreet Saluja, Jeff Goldfarb, Akhil Sharma, Arul Louis, Madhusmita Bora, Saurav Pathak, Amitava Kumar, and Arun Nava for their time, invaluable suggestions, and close reading. Mira Kamdar and Suketu Mehta provided much direction and needed encouragement during a writing seminar. The glory of this finished product remains collective; all errors mine.

I lovingly thank my brothers, Sanjib and Rahul, who have provided comic relief and unconditional support throughout my life and throughout this process. May we continue to turn the notion of "confused desis" on its head.

Finally, I thank my parents, to whom this is dedicated. Their migration to America inspired more than this book. The courage they've collectively demonstrated and the success they've equally achieved serve as the framework for all I undertake. May my mother's generosity and my father's intellectual zeal continue to guide my life and work.

Suburban Sahibs

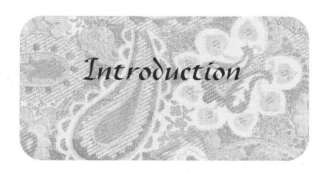

Introduction

My earliest childhood memory is of an immigrant navigating suburbia—literally. She was my mother, Nirmala Kalita. In 1978, my parents bought their first home in Massapequa, a working-class town on Long Island; the down payment was made with savings from her night shift at Burger King. My mother was left with no choice but to learn to drive. As she nervously steered our newly purchased yet secondhand orange Vega, I sat in the back, my two-year-old frame strapped into a car seat.

So my confession begins: I am a product of the very subject I write about on the pages that follow. My father emigrated from India to New York City in 1971, sent for my mother and elder brother the following year, and began to climb a corporate ladder from the bottom: a temp job at Citibank. Their move into a $40,000 split-level home on Long Island thrust my brother and me into a school system where we were the only nonwhites, as far as we could tell. We endured little blatant racism but plenty of questions about just "what kind" of Indian we were. "What tribe?" one teacher asked. Quickly, as the children of immigrants tend to do, I became two Mitras. The one at home spoke Assamese, ate with her little hands, and slept tucked between two parents in a king-size bed. The one at school spoke in a thick Long Island accent, dreamed of a family past as storied as Laura Ingalls Wilder's, and vacillated between the black Cabbage Patch Kid and the white one, settling on the latter. I grew distressed if my two worlds collided, as they inevitably did. Before friends came over, I sprayed several rounds of air freshener to rid our house of its pungent cooking odor; I never smelled the scent my brothers and I dubbed "IFS," for Indian Food Smell, but knew it existed because my classmates told me so. When my mother wore a sari to school graduations and ballet recitals, I secretly wished she wore a business suit or floral dress like the other moms.

In 1985, my father was promoted to a vice presidency at Citibank and transferred to Puerto Rico. Although we protested it, the move was a blessing to our fledgling cultural identities. My brothers (by this time, I had two) and I encountered newfound otherness virtually every day as we wore the metaphorical hats of the Indians we were at home, the white suburbanites we once had attempted to be, newcomers to an island colony that "belonged" to the United States yet somehow didn't, and members of an elite class created by an employer who paid our country club membership and private school tuition. Once again, we quickly adapted ourselves to the new world we were living in, eventually learning to translate and navigate its components on our own terms.

Transferred back to the mainland in 1988, my family began looking for a house in the tri-state area. Now that they had money to spend, my parents based their decisions exclusively on good school districts and proximity to a direct train line to New York City. New Jersey was the clear choice.

Apparently, a lot of other families like ours had had the same idea. As we rode in rental car after rental car to look at one four-bedroom Colonial after another, settling finally on a home in West Windsor, my brothers and I would count the Indians along the New Jersey Turnpike. Not until undertaking this book more than a decade later would I embark on a journey to discover just why they came.

This book traces the evolution of the suburb. New arrivals once viewed it as the destination of their journey. For many, home ownership in a place with good schools and soccer leagues, strip malls and picket fences, signified the completion of the American Dream. To get there, they had to toil for years in cities, ride subways, scrimp and save. But as city economies declined, manufacturing jobs moved, and chain migration increased, the immigrant experience in America was redefined. Today, the suburbs have become a launching pad for the newcomer's journey in America. I tell this story through exploring the migration to central New Jersey of three waves of Indian immigrant groups, represented by three families: the Kotharis, Patels, and Sarmas. I spent two years interviewing them and following their lives, using no formal surveys or questionnaires, just a pen, a notebook, and observation.

I met Pradip Kothari in the spring of 2000 when the idea of documenting the explosion of South Asian immigrants in central Jersey was still a nebulous one. I was a student at Columbia University's Graduate School of Journalism taking a course taught by Samuel G. Freedman, the award-winning author of several books including *Small Victories* and *Jew versus Jew*. Sam wanted me to unlearn my own experience as the daughter of immigrants in New Jersey and try to see the place anew. So I called up Pradip Kothari, president of the Indo-American Cultural Society, and asked him to help me do that.

Pradip's was the first interview I did. We met on a Sunday morning at his travel agency; the office was closed, but people came in in a steady stream. They were not customers but fellow Indians seeking help, advice, or support. Pradip—I could never get used to calling him "Peter" as everyone else did—rarely missed a beat, stopping our conversation to tend to them and then turning back to me to finish the sentence he had just interrupted. During our meeting, I caught glimpses of his daughters, Payal and Toral, who came in to ask for money as they headed to the mall. We only smiled and exchanged hellos, but their presence helped me see Pradip as not only a community leader but also a father and husband.

There is a danger in interviewing people who have been interviewed often. From prior research on the area, I knew reporters often turned to Pradip as their first, perhaps only, source on the Indian community; over the years, it seemed, his answers grew more and more prepared. I wondered if he would allow me to go deeper with him, if he would speak in more than just quotes.

In Pradip's family, I saw much of my own. They were the so-called success stories that fill immigrant suburbia. Arrival in the suburbs and the accompanying multistory homes and cars were the clear signs of "making it." But what made Pradip and his wife Nandini's story compelling from our first meetings was that they seemed to want much more. Despite the couple's prominence at various Indian functions and festivals, they appeared somewhat sidelined by many facets of American life. I could feel that Pradip was on the verge of doing something about it. When I first met him, however, it was not clear what that might be.

Many of those who came behind the immigrants of the Kotharis' generation also appeared sidelined—but in a much different way. Easier to spot, these immigrants pumped gas, walked miles along busy roads without sidewalks to the train station, crammed eight into a car at 5:00 A.M. to get to work, and ignored the exasperated sighs of annoyance at their accents or perhaps lack of English altogether. I saw cashiers at Burger King who had spent years behind the counter serving Whoppers and fries, unlike my mother, whose two years of earnings helped buy her family a home to ensure she would never have to take such orders again.

"McMansions," as planners dub virtual starter castles marketed to soccer moms and dads, are not an option for those who flip or serve burgers for a living. As more working-class immigrants from South Asia call the suburbs of central Jersey home, those immigrants have been hard pressed to find affordable housing. Families of four or more not uncommonly live in a one-bedroom apartment, in cramped conditions more reminiscent of cities. To witness this phenomenon, I needed to look no further than Hilltop Estates, a sprawling apartment complex housing mainly South Asian immigrants situated just off Oak Tree Road—turn at the Dairy Queen and go past a bowling alley. Location is what motivated dwellers to move into Hilltop's five hundred units. The main thoroughfare of Indian stores on Oak Tree Road is not exactly a stone's throw away, but to a new transplant's legs, the half-mile distance is certainly walkable. So is the mile to the Metro Park train station, where many Hilltop residents trek daily to at dawn and fro at dusk.

Unlike other housing complexes, which boast billboard signs—"If you lived here, you'd be home by now!"—and large bold squares in newspaper classifieds, Hilltop needs no publicity. "It's a landmark. Indians bound for the U.S., who haven't even heard of JFK Airport, know all about Hilltop Apartments in Edison where they will be staying," Sunil Mehta, manager of the complex, told *Little India* magazine.

So one weekend afternoon, a few days after I had first met with Pradip, I found myself roaming Hilltop. Rather than knock on random doors, I headed for the complex's laundry room, thinking that residents there would have nothing better to do than talk to me. Outside, I met Kajal Patel, a reticent teenager who seemed to bear more burdens than girls her age should, and there began my relationship with her family.

6 Suburban Sahibs

The Patels have lived in Edison since 1990. When I met them, Kajal's father, Harish, worked at Bradlees, while her mother worked at a retail distribution company packing boxes. They struggled to support their family on their slightly above minimum-wage salaries but humbled me with their generosity, buying my favorite sweets and juice drinks if they knew I was coming over. At first, they said little about Zankhana, Kajal's elder sister and the face gracing most photos lining the family's living room. They slowly opened up about her: she had eloped and moved to Rochester with a Sikh cabdriver she met in Hilltop; now, gradually, she was reentering their lives. Eventually, the Patels even put me in touch with Zankhana to get her side. More often, though, my time with the Patels was spent discussing job searches and money woes.

In the Patels, I saw a new side of Indian America and a side of suburbia devoid of picket fences. Zankhana and Kajal had grown up handing their paychecks to their father each week. It reminded me of a poem I'd read, "Indian Movie, New Jersey," by Chitra Banerjee Divakaruni, its last lines referring to an "America that was supposed to be." Indeed, the more Harish Patel opened up to me, the more elusive the American Dream seemed, the more it seemed like just a dream.

To be sure, that America did reveal itself to some. They were the newly arrived, highly skilled Indians who earned salaries closer to six figures than not, who were greeted with limousine rides at airports, who knew what Guess and Gap were, whose knowledge of computer programming languages from JAVA to COBAL to C++ paved their entry to the United States. The lives they "escaped" in India were those that included maids, chauffeurs, and lunches and dinners at five-star hotels. This group thought it had America pretty well figured out. Yet I saw an America that was ambivalent about how to treat these new arrivals, allowing them in only if they promised not to stay longer than six years.

In techie parlance, they are known as H-1B's, referring to the category of visa under which they gain entry to the United States. I met many along Oak Tree Road in my research, but the family I eventually tapped for this book I met at a dinner party in my own parents' home. My parents and some of their friends were helping organize an annual convention of the Assamese community in North America. Assam, the region in northeastern India my family hails from, exports very few emigrants to America, unlike Punjab, Gujarat, and increasingly states in South India like Karnataka, Andhra Pradesh, and Tamil Nadu. Each year, the few Assamese expatriates who are here gather for a weekend convention of singing, dancing, and socializing.

As I walked into the basement, where a chorus had begun practicing, one male voice stood out from the rest. I stopped because this guy actually sounded good, not like the creaking, croaking amateurs I'd heard my whole life. Later in the evening, I learned he was Sankumani Sarma and had been in the United States for less than a year with his wife, Shravani, and two-year-old-son, Arunabh, known as Chiku at home. Upon arrival in the United States, they moved straight to a housing development in Edison.

Hearing about my interest in their new hometown, Shravani and Sanku quickly turned the questioning around on me, asking me about my upbringing, my feelings of belonging neither here nor there, even my predictions on whether the tech boom would last. As the Sarmas left several hours later, I noticed that Chiku carried a water gun he had found in the basement among my younger brother's old playthings. Shravani was trying to convince him to leave it behind.

"That's okay," I offered. "My brother's too old to play with it anymore."

"Oh, no," she said. "He's not allowed to play with guns. He sees enough violence on television here."

After I shut the door, her words echoed through my head. I knew I wanted to talk more to her and Sanku about the America they had encountered.

In the Kotharis, Patels, and Sarmas, I saw a book. Its characters came to me in the most organic of ways, unknown to each other, sharing in common only the home they knew then and the home they know now.

The backdrop of these families' tales of migration and transformation is a seemingly typical place: the American suburb. Central New Jersey, however, is anything but typical. Amid the suburban sprawl that straddles the New Jersey Turnpike and Garden State Parkway, the region houses one of the largest communities of South Asians in the United States. Tangible signs of that distinction are everywhere. In Edison neighborhoods around dinnertime, the smell of curries and cardamom wafts over freshly manicured lawns. In the commercial center in the Iselin section of Woodbridge, specifically along Oak Tree Road, parking is nonexistent, so Toyotas and Hondas double-park and blast the latest Bollywood songs. Hindu and Sikh temples dot highways and side roads, carved out of former homes, churches, office spaces, and toy factories. On weekend mornings, the clapping and chanting inside reach one's ears even before entering.

Often the butt of jokes, New Jersey is the most densely populated state in the union. Central Jersey, roughly defined as encompassing Middlesex, Somerset, Hunterdon, and some parts of Mercer and Monmouth counties, is a commuter's dream with a complex system of highways and parkways, overpasses and underpasses, that can send drivers north toward New York, south toward Philadelphia, east toward Staten Island, west toward industrial parks and suburban sprawl. As the population of the area surges, traffic has grown ever more snarled, class sizes have exceeded the state average, and open spaces have become a rarity. Larger townships, such as Woodbridge in Middlesex County, hang on to neighborhood names such as Iselin, Colonia, Avenel, and Fords. Housing stock throughout the region runs a gamut from older Cape Cod–style homes selling for less than $200,000 to million-dollar mansions, which sit on former farmlands. In a common practice, developments and streets are named after the farming family from which the tract was purchased. Newer immigrants have their Oak Tree Roads, while Irish bars, Elks Lodges, and pasta dinners at firehouses provide pastimes for residents who have been around longer. They wave flags and cheer on high school bands and local politicians at quaint parades marching past whatever is defined as a downtown in suburbia. In South Plainfield, a Middlesex County suburb known for its Labor Day celebration, the parade route winds past the borough hall, the rescue squad, the firehouse, and the public library.

Perhaps Edison is the central New Jersey town best known among Americans for being the place where Thomas Alva Edison invented the lightbulb in 1876. Over the next hundred years, what was then known as the township of Raritan would name high schools, streets, monuments, and eventually itself after the famous inventor. The township seal includes the motto "Let There Be Light." Historic records depict a man who toiled away in his Menlo Park laboratory into the early morning hours and would venture to Perth Amboy occasionally for fishing trips. Even by late nineteenth-century standards, central New Jersey could be considered quaint. To commemorate Edison's invention, for example, the first string of Christmas lights was lit in the Menlo Park section of Raritan Township in 1879 on bare fields. That year, tourists invaded the town to gawk at the lights display.

The next century saw much growth in what used to be rural Middlesex County. Companies such as Ford, Revlon, American Can, the New York Times Company, and Johnson & Johnson opened headquarters or assembly plants, and workers flocked to the region. For much of the twentieth century, white ethnics defined Middlesex County: Italians, Hungarians, and Irish. In the 1960s, a U.S. military installation along the Raritan River was shut down, prompting much protest from residents over the loss of six hundred jobs. Replacing the installation, though, was Raritan Center, an industrial park where tens of thousands of people in hundreds of companies work. Companies and developers alike found its thirty-two square miles of mostly open land incredibly appealing and profitable. Unlike other suburbs, Edison has no main street or downtown; its geographic center is literally the separate town of Metuchen. Otherwise, Edison's history frames it as a quintessentially American town.

In Edison and Woodbridge today, residents fiercely hold on to the identity of the sections in which they live. "McMansions" and sprawling colonial- or Cape Cod–style, cookie-cutter homes define North Edison and the Colonia section of Woodbridge. The growth of such communities over the last ten years has led demographers to label Middlesex, Monmouth, Somerset, and Hunterdon counties New Jersey's "wealth belt." Indeed, immigrants helped fuel the trend. Between 1990 and 2000, New Jersey's Indian population grew more than 100 percent from 79,440 to 169,180. In Edison, the Indian population nearly tripled during the same period, from 6,000 to nearly 17,000. At the same time, though, the overall population in Edison increased by just 9,000.

Despite the extensive historical records on the inventor and town's namesake, little besides the census documents the mass immigration of Indians to the town. "You didn't see this coming. You saw it happen," explains Edison's amateur historian David Sheehan. The first generation of suburban Indians like the Kotharis started American life in a city—New York or Jersey City, primarily. Later waves, however, emigrated directly from the subcontinent to the suburbs, often staying with friends or relatives. Today, suburban areas like central New Jersey serve as the backdrop to both the beginning and end of the search for the American Dream.

The first influx of Indian immigrants arrived as a direct result of the Immigration and Nationality Act of 1965, which eliminated racial criteria and gave every country a quota of 20,000 people. These immigrants often took jobs that Americans turned down because of low pay or remote location. By the 1980 census, of the 400,000 Indians in the United States, 11 percent of the men were physicians, while 17 percent were engineers, architects, or surveyors. Eight percent of the women were physicians, and 7 percent were nurses. Most entered through New York City, clustering in neighborhoods like Jackson Heights and Flushing, sections of Queens. Others found themselves the only doctors or nurses on staff in states such as Alabama, Mississippi, and Kansas.

In the 1970s and 1980s, Indians were widely scattered; often there would only be one or two Indian families—who might also be the only people of color—in an entire neighborhood or town. Also in this time period, many Indians who had lived in Africa sought refuge in the United States after violence and political instability in Uganda, Kenya, and other African nations led them to flee.

Laws changed again in 1986, allowing immigration based on lotteries and family sponsorships, thus inviting migrants without sought-after skills to enter the United States. The new, larger wave doubled the Indian population to 815,000 in the 1990 census, most fitting in with the traditional immigrant profile of shopkeepers, restaurant owners, newsstand vendors, and cabdrivers. Nonetheless, the strengths that Indian migrants brought with them were their education and knowledge of English. According to the Center for Immigration Studies, a conservative think tank in Washington, D.C., only 3 percent of Indian arrivals lack a high school education, while about 20 percent of the U.S. population overall does. And 75 percent of Indian immigrants who work are college graduates, compared to about a third of the U.S. population overall. Census data do not yet gauge the impact of high-tech workers of Indian origin, but it can be assumed they have a bachelor's degree, and anecdotal evidence suggests a master's degree is more often the norm.

In central New Jersey, the commercial center for Indians is a street that cuts through the Oak Tree section of Edison and the

Iselin section of Woodbridge. In the early 1980s, little distinguished this strip of garden-apartment complexes and mom-and-pop stores from any other suburban downtown. There was Jimmy's Meat Market, a competing Polish butcher, a hardware store, a five-and-dime, several gas stations, and a drive-in theater on the Edison side of the road. Today, there are sari shops, restaurants, jewelry and electronics boutiques, doctors' offices, and auto-repair garages with names like "Deepa," "Patel," and "Singh." Psychic readers and astrologers are plentiful, their services most needed when couples hope to set the most auspicious of wedding dates.

According to the 1990 census, nearly 20,000 Asian Indians—as they are called in the census—were among the 671,000 residents in Middlesex County. The reasons Indians have been drawn to Middlesex County are simple. During the 1980s, these areas—like many suburbs—offered good schools, a low crime rate, and a commute to New York City of less than one hour. Quite simply, immigrants wanted what most people moving to the suburbs want.

Yet tensions among the Indians and longtime residents of Middlesex County do exist, thickening during times of economic recession. The owners of mom-and-pop stores along Oak Tree Road often complain the Indians are driving them out. Indian business owners say there is more of a demand for the specialized services they can provide. They also point to the growth of chains and superstores in their communities as factors that compete with independently owned hardware, discount, and grocery stores.

Today, strained relations still exist between Indians and the leaders of the community they inhabit. Edison Township's government has been accused of not reflecting its diversity; as it entered the twenty-first century and as I embarked on this project, of its thousand municipal employees, just a handful were Indian.

Even within the South Asian community, relations tend to become strained; people are divided by language, region, caste, class, even generation. Most Indians of my generation have heard themselves described as an "ABCD," for American Born Confused Desi. ("Desi," the slang term for South Asians who live away from the subcontinent, is from the Hindi for "country.") The acronym has even been stretched to Z: "American Born Confused Desi, Emigrated From Gujarat, Housed In Jersey, Keeping Lotsa Motels, Named Omkarnath Patel, Quickly Reached Success Through Underhanded Vicious Ways, Xenophobic Yet Zestful."

Indians upset with this characterization—or perhaps cognizant of their presence and success in the suburbs—responded with "American Born Confused Desi, Emigrated From Gujarat, Housed in Jersey, Kids Learning Medicine, Now Owning Property, Quite Reasonable Salary, Two Uncles Visiting, White Xenophobia Yet Zestful."

As the potential butt of an ABCD joke, I debate its accuracy. But both versions of the joke demonstrate that New Jersey has been a central part of Indians' history in America. The 1999 yearbook for J. P. Stevens High School boasts seven pages of graduating Patels alone. The Yellow Pages for both Edison and Woodbridge have more Patels than Smiths and more Shahs than Joneses.

In the late nineteenth century, tourists descended on Edison to see its Christmas lights display. Today, from New Jersey, New York, Connecticut, and Pennsylvania, more than 60,000 Indians pass through the massive white tent set up on a lawn next to Raritan Center for their own colorful festival of Navratri.

This is where our story begins.

For the purpose of narration, I focus on a period of about one year, beginning with Navratri in October 2000 and ending with Election Day of 2001. Interwoven are the individual subjects' stories of coming to America, or "Amrika" as it is known in India, and the years leading up to the time period I focus upon. If there was ever a year to chronicle the lives of South Asians in America, this was it. There was the presidential election of 2000, after which for many weeks nobody knew who would be president. Days after President George W. Bush was sworn in, an earthquake rocked Gujarat, killing thousands and moving many in New Jersey to mobilize relief efforts. It was the year when the country's longest period of economic prosperity came to a grinding halt. The dot-com bubble burst, the stock market tanked, and the pink slips came home. Then the date that needs no explanation—Tuesday, September 11, 2001. As the World Trade Center and Pentagon were attacked, many desis walked a tightrope over loyalties to here and there. Suddenly, they feared their fellow Americans and a backlash against their brown skin. Yet they also feared the same enemy in terrorism and war, which many had sought haven from on U.S. soil. And of course, there are the vicissitudes that mark each character's own personal journey: Toral Kothari's high school graduation; Harish Patel's search for employment; Sankumani Sarma's luck with the stock market.

For the sake of accuracy, individual members of the families reviewed portions of the manuscript with the understanding they could only correct errors in fact. All dialogue that is presented was personally witnessed by me or recounted to me by at least one participant. Dialogue or thoughts that could not be fully remembered appear in italics.

In the beginning, I hoped my subjects' pursuit of the American Dream would shed some light on the estimated 1.7 million Indians living in the United States. Instead, what I found was that their experience offered a window into what America has become: a nation of suburbs, a nation of immigrants. Their story could easily be mine, or yours.

Prologue: A New Year

Under a canopy tent, thousands step and twirl and skip in sync, silks flailing, skirts swishing, jeans scraping. Bare, pedicured, bejeweled feet alongside Nikes and Timberlands hit the carpet for just a moment before the next step takes over, picking up speed with each beat of the drums and the melodious sounds and high pitches of home. Here, in suburban New Jersey, the 7-Eleven cashier and Amoco gas station attendant become dancing kings with whom bankers and computer programmers struggle to keep pace.

It is the night of October 7, 2000, one of the nights of Navratri, a Hindu festival commemorating good's conquest of evil. The tent's canvas walls encompass a heated area three times the size of a football field but can't keep the crowds within from shivering or blowing clouds as they breathe and speak. The teenagers with their North Face puffy jackets keep them on as they dance, brown faces eventually dripping with sweat, arms pumping out of the thick material of their outerwear. To stay warm, the others also dance fast or sip chai sold at stalls manned by mustachioed men and hairnetted women.

In the center of the makeshift hall, she sits. The icon of the eight-armed goddess, known as Amba to Gujaratis and as Durga to Bengalis and other North Indians, gives a reason to convene on autumn weekends. Each dance symbolically circles her, the feminine manifestation of God. At 2:00 A.M., worshipers gather around as close as they can and light a fire and pray for peace. To take Amba's blessing, their hands approach the flame, just close enough to feel the warmth, then graze the tops of their heads.

And they scurry back to dance some more. Those who don't dance simply watch from the sideline bleachers, order plates of salty spicy snacks such as samosa chaat, bhel puri, or pau bhaji, or comb through racks of salwar kameezes, saris, and lehenga cholis, perhaps to buy an outfit for next week.

For a moment, those who left India may feel they never really did, from the wives who followed their husbands' dreams to the educated who learned to make doughnuts and count change in nickels and dimes to the children who search for the scent of Grandmother's sandalwood soap in the faint, faded, foreign words of a blue aerogram. Tonight, they transport themselves back to those festival nights when Papa carried them home and sleep was so sound they didn't feel the scratch of the mosquito net against their bare legs as Ma erected it around the bed they shared. She remembers laughing at the neighbor's son as he brought her a cup of sugarcane juice seasoned with salt and spices in between dances. He remembers the tough talk of teenagers, his first smoke, and a resolve to outdream the others.

Underneath the tent, they relive those moments, taste them, see them, hear them, *remember*. Beyond the tent's walls lies the evidence of newly forged frontiers. Steps away, a parking lot filled with Toyota Camrys and Honda Accords and sport utility vehicles. Yards away, the entrance to the New Jersey Turnpike. Miles away, houses equipped with central heating and air-conditioning.

Three-car garages or perhaps none. Mortgages or dreams of qualifying for one. Student loans, credit card debt. Home as they know it now, half a world away from the home they knew then.

Behind these memories, the music, the movements, is a fleet of volunteers and organizers spearheaded by one man who appears to be everywhere yet nowhere. Pradip "Peter" Kothari dances a few steps for the cameras, then leaves the floor. He checks in with a vendor selling religious statues, then swiftly talks to the next one selling international calling plans. At center stage, he takes the microphone, then hands it off to a politician or visiting artist. Each year, Pradip tries to create more of what he remembers from a memory where nostalgia reigns.

Inevitably, his mind drifts back four decades to his college days on the campus of Maharajah Sayajirao University in Baroda, a city in the Indian province of Gujarat and his hometown. The son of politically active members of India's Congress Party, Pradip spent more time organizing rallies and festivals than in the classroom. His parents, concerned about his lack of responsibility and carefree ways, sent him to America to join his sister in 1972. For a decade, he stayed out of the limelight, studying nuclear medicine, traveling to Gujarat to marry Nandini, bringing her back, having two daughters. When he opened his business, a travel agency on Oak Tree Road, and someone threw eggs and rocks at his windows, Pradip organized a merchants' association. Once again, he found himself organizing festivals. His Navratri celebrations first outgrew the auditoriums of local schools, then public halls, then moved to the massive tent with no boundaries. What he has created in Edison, New Jersey, on the fields of Raritan Center, one of the largest industrial parks in the country, is the single largest celebration of Navratri beyond India's borders.

Navratri literally means "nine nights," for the novena devotees offer prayers, visit temples, and celebrate the force of nature, worshiped in the iconic form of Amba. The circular dance, garba, traditionally takes place around an earthenware pot as a singer and drummer perform, first slowly, then faster and faster. The pot rarely makes an appearance in U.S. adaptations of Navratri, however. Further, most Indian Americans spread their celebration out over weekend nights so children don't miss school and parents don't miss work. After a break, a folk dance known as daandia raas begins, in which pairs of men and women face each other and clang sticks to a beat, then whirl around to face a new partner. Traditionally, the sticks are made of hollowed-out wood, but at Pradip's extravaganza, vendors sell thick plastic rods that clang in colors of hot pink, neon green, and electric blue.

His Navratri has had its share of battles over its decade-long run. Indeed, its roots lie in conflict. Pradip started to organize the festivals in 1990 with Prabhu Patel. That very year, the two had a public falling-out—Pradip accused Prabhu of wanting to work within the system, while he preferred to challenge it—and Pradip went on to stage his own festivals under the auspices of a newly created organization. Attendees often wonder whether Pradip's endless hunger to expand the festival exponentially stems from the public rivalry between the two men.

Through its history, the festival has been mired in controversies from within and outside the Indian community. For years, neighbors complained the loud music and late hours kept them up all night. A battle between festival organizers and Edison Township ended in a settlement—but only after six years of legal haranguing. A federal judge ruled a curfew that had been imposed unconstitutional. Organizers still keep a Radio Shack sound meter around to ensure that the decibels stay between 90 and 100, comparable to most nightclubs.

In Pradip's mind, he likened the township's accusations to the rocks the bigots threw at his travel agency's windows—a racist message saying he and his people were not welcomed. "I am one hundred percent sure that if Bruce Springsteen came to

Edison and played loud music, the town would throw a great party for him," he said in 1995. "Every community has a right to carry out cultural events and pass their heritage to the next generation. We don't want special treatment, just fair treatment."

Within the Indian community, critics claim the festival is more of a commercial venture than a religious event. One even dubbed it a "Hindu *Jesus Christ Superstar.*" Another says it's a simple way for Pradip to preserve his "Godfather" status.

It's clear Pradip does not lack ego. His name graces everything related to Navratri, from the souvenir program to the advertisements that adorn the hall to the plaques given to politicians and guest artists from India. In the months before the tents go up, his travel agency in the "Little India" section of town becomes festival headquarters. Contracts for lighting, heating, and security guards heap on his desk, alongside tickets and itineraries.

Dressed in a suit with a massive, multicolored ribbon denoting him someone important, Pradip's stocky frame wanders between backstage and the security trailer. His pace is brisk, his face weary from the night before when he collapsed into bed around 5:00 A.M. This morning, he arrived at 8:00 to do it all again.

"Everything okay?" Pradip asks one of a half-dozen security guards stationed out front. After a decade, Pradip's eyes are trained to spot the ones who arrive drunk or high, or sober yet looking for trouble. His daughters' friends fear him year-round; behind his back, they call him "Big Pete." Tonight, as on most nights, someone will be kicked out. This is so expected that it's not even gossiped about anymore.

As Navratri's popularity has grown among teenagers and young adults, festival organizers have reported fights and underage drinking. During Navratri 1999, an e-mail message circulated saying a woman was raped in the parking lot; Pradip, along with Edison police, insists independent investigation yielded no proof of the allegation.

Pradip relaxes a bit more tonight than other nights. New Jersey governor Christie Whitman isn't scheduled to stop by for a few weeks. Nor is her two-time competition for the job, Woodbridge mayor James McGreevey, a Democrat. Bollywood heartthrob Sanjay Kapoor will be here in two weeks. Pradip breathes easier because the bigger names always need bigger men for security purposes. Tonight, the only dignitaries Pradip plans to put onstage are council members from nearby Piscataway. Inevitably, they'll look at the crowd and wave. Perhaps they'll clasp their hands together and try to pronounce "Namaste" or "Jai Hind." The two terms—the former a greeting, the latter a rally cry meaning "Long live India"—have suddenly become staples for any elected official in Middlesex County.

Pradip wishes they knew more. Increasingly, he is bothered by politicians' lack of willingness to put Indians on their advisory committees and town councils. *Can't they see how the county is changing?* In the beginning, Pradip had limited his own involvement to the Indian community. Now, he is a member of the Kiwanis, Lions, and Key clubs and serves on the Human Relations Council. Last year, he and Nandini traveled with McGreevey to India. They also joined former governor Jim Florio and his wife, Lucinda, to raise money for the YMCA's expansion of a facility adjacent to the Jewish Community Center of Middlesex County. But it didn't seem enough. In the beginning, Pradip was just happy to get them onstage and shake their hands as the flashes went off from the ethnic presses. Lately, though, he's been wanting more, and he's not sure how to get it.

By 10:00 P.M., Nandini and the girls arrive, wearing one of the dozens of ornate Indian outfits they purchase each year for this season. They separate as soon as they enter, their mother to the VIP section of the dance floor nearest the stage, the girls to, in their words, "scope."

"FOBs, preps, and thugs," quickly assesses twenty-year-old Payal. Toral nods, craning her neck for the guy she likes.

Among desi youth, Payal's words need no translation. FOBs are the guys just arrived from India, or maybe they've been here a few years; if they still possess accents and tailored plaid shirts, the "fresh off the boat" label holds. Preps wear plaid shirts, too, but theirs come from Gap or Banana Republic; their cologne is Polo Sport or Versace Blue Jeans, and their tortoiseshell glasses are from Guess. Thugs wear their Tommy Hilfiger jeans below their hips and big, big shoes. They shave their heads and adorn themselves in puffy jackets, ski hats, and sunglasses.

Payal is in no mood for any of them and heads for the dance floor quicker than usual. At five-foot-eight, her slim frame topped with a bun, she stands taller than most of the other girls. She performs the steps in a perfunctory manner, a smile noticeably absent from her face. So much consumes her mind lately. Payal just moved back home and transferred to Kean University in Union, New Jersey, after two years spent at St. John's University in Queens. One December day last year, in the middle of her finals, Payal was napping in her dorm room decorated in Winnie-the-Pooh collectibles and posters with slogans like "All I need to know about life I learned from my girlfriends." She awoke to the sight of a stranger rifling through her jewelry box. When she asked who he was, he said he was looking for "Christine," then left. Payal reported the incident to police and discovered there had been a handful of similar break-ins across campus. She provided a written statement to police but never told her parents, fearing they'd worry about her even more. Her grade point average in her first year did nothing to make her parents proud. The next year, busy with her new friends and still exploring the city, she never raised her GPA as she had pledged at the beginning of the semester. In early July, a desi boy she had been casually dating was killed in a car accident. She didn't attend the funeral, didn't tell her parents. Over the summer, Payal decided to transfer and move back home.

The only one she could bring herself to talk to about the events of last year was Toral. Mom suspected something, but Dad didn't really discuss dating with them. Payal and Toral often joke that they have a "don't ask, don't tell" policy with their father. It was just better to keep it inside, Payal reasoned.

So on this, the eve of an Indian new year, Payal tries to put the past out of her mind. So far, it already feels like she'll get a lot more studying done at Kean. Living with Mom and Dad isn't so bad. Besides, now she has her car back. That beats waiting for the Q30 or Q31 bus from Queens to Manhattan any day.

In the tent where vendors set up shop, Toral finally finds the object of her latest crush, a spectacled, lanky Indian boy swathed in a bulky yellow winter jacket. Payal had already labeled him "not cute," but Toral doesn't care. She longs for the perfect senior year. Maybe this will be the year she finds a boyfriend, her first. Or at least a prom date she actually cares about. Toral just found out she is the Colonia High School Class of 2001 salutatorian. Her family isn't surprised. After all, this is the same girl who earned a 1450 on her SAT on the Saturday morning after a night of dancing and partying at Navratri until 4:00 A.M. School comes so much easier for her than for Payal.

After a few minutes of talking to her crush and other friends—the "desi crew," as the girls call them—Toral lines up behind Payal, in their usual spot in the circle immediately surrounding Amba. Toral, petite and pretty, doesn't miss a step.

In the VIP area cordoned off by security guards and metal fences, Nandini Kothari also dances, slower than her girls. She's dancing with the men and women who work in Pradip's travel agency; a perk of working there is not having to pay the $20 nightly fee for VIP admission. In years past, Nandini used to help Pradip run the festivals, but work had gotten so hectic, and she didn't have the patience anymore. *All those Indian women gossiping about who was marrying who, how much this piece of gold jewelry cost, how much the Patels or Shahs had donated to the temple.*

Nandini's job as a medical records supervisor takes her to three hospitals in three separate counties in New Jersey; she has recently been promoted. She doesn't have time to care about trivial matters. Still, at these functions, it becomes obvious to Nandini that most Indians still see her as Pradip's wife and the cohost of the evening. Pradip himself drags her onstage and asks her to make small talk with the chief guests or dance with them. She arrives at the festivals most nights bearing Thermoses of steaming tea, made milky and sweet for the visiting artists to warm up themselves and their voices between acts. October in New Jersey feels nothing like October in Bombay. Nandini indulges Pradip when she can, but lately the functions seem to be piling up.

Yet Nandini knows the alternative all too well. *Would she rather be a housewife in India?* she often asks herself. *Sitting home all day, watching the kids, supervising cooks and maids and gardeners.*

The Kotharis, once dubbed the "festival family" in a newspaper article, are scattered under the tent for most of the night. Sometimes, all four of their cars are parked in the lot, a sign of a particularly eventful day that ends in their separate arrivals. But at 2:00 A.M., they gather as a family to pray during aarti, when offerings are made to Amba. Payal usually holds the tray of flickering candles and circles it one way, then the other. Pradip and Nandini mouth the words to the Hindu prayer that the bands sing. Toral knows them, too; she recited them as the little girl whose hair Pradip combed into pigtails and recites them now as a teenager who gels her curls into place on her own. Maybe next year, when she's in college, she won't be able to come back. But for now, the family is together; for these few moments all four seem to find themselves united—praying among thousands.

Hail, master, lord of the universe
who removes in a moment the troubles
of devotees and the sufferings
of the poor.

One who meditates on you gets the fruit
Sorrow is removed from mind and heart
Happiness and wealth come to the home
Pain is wiped from the body.

You are my mother and father
In whom I take refuge
No other than you do I accept
Of whom I accept everything.

As she sings this prayer under the tent, Kajal Patel stands not with her family—her parents are home asleep—but a trio of friends, Alpa and Ritu and Pritesh. After the prayer, they take prasad, a mixture of nuts and sugar cubes that represents a sacred offering to God, and later shared among devotees as a sacrament. When the festival opened on September 22, Kajal didn't go. "This isn't the religious weekend," she'd said. "They only open it this early to make money."

But tonight is the real thing; neither Kajal nor her father has any qualms about her attendance. Still, Kajal's father, Harish, feels that the festival stands for commercialism, tainting his religion with U.S. dollars. Maybe Harish will come later in the month, but he never stays long. He prefers to pray at Shree Ram Mandir, a temple across from the Metuchen train station, on Sunday evenings. Besides, Navratri tickets cost $15, a luxury for the Patel family. Harish earns $8 per hour, and Kajal's mother, Kapila, earns the same; she does get overtime, albeit compulsory. Kajal's ticket cost one-tenth of the weekly paycheck she earns as a checkout girl at ShopRite. She buys her ticket in advance to save the extra $2 charged for paying at the door. Kajal never complains, though, simply saying, "I know my dad will find something better soon."

Tonight, she wears her favorite blue lehenga, ornate and dazzling, but it's the same one she wore to a Navratri two years ago. Kajal only occasionally buys new clothes in the shops along Oak Tree Road, instead waiting for her uncles or family friends to visit India and bring her something back. "It's cheaper that way," she reasons.

Indeed, Kajal has been raised to be practical. She dances just a few circles away from Payal and Toral Kothari, the same steps to the same song. But their worlds are so clearly different. Kajal, a sophomore at Middlesex County College, hands a portion of her $150 in take-home pay to her father each week, saving the rest for gas and school expenses. She sleeps on the couch in the family's apartment, leaving the bedroom for her parents. Tonight, she'll slip in around 4:00 A.M. She's not usually allowed to be out this late, but for Navratri, Papa makes an exception.

As Kajal dances, teaches Alpa the steps, and chats with friends, Harish lies awake in the family's one-bedroom apartment in the Hilltop apartment complex off Oak Tree Road, consumed in thought. Harish Patel works at Bradlee's, a discount store with a distribution center in Edison, as an accounts clerk. In February 1999, Bradlee's emerged from a bankruptcy protection filing with a $270 million bank loan to help it rebuild. But in the face of the competition from the behemoth and ever-expanding Wal-Mart, it looks as if Bradlee's will sink into bankruptcy yet again. Discount retailer Caldor certainly hadn't survived, and Ames is in the middle of layoffs and store closings. In this fall Harish remains hopeful for his employer but not overly optimistic. Sales at Bradlee's have been steadily declining, blamed on the cold summer and warm winter. Harish hears that his job depends on the success of this Christmas season. He's also heard Home Depot or Kohl's might bail his company out.

He hopes someone comes to the rescue. The family's lease is up at the end of the month, and Harish wants to get them out of this apartment where his daughter must sleep on the couch, where the door handles fall off and the stains on the wall deepen day by day.

Their move to Hilltop a decade ago was supposed to be temporary. So was his hourly-wage job; so was the fact that he sent his wife to work; so was the few thousand Harish put on his credit cards that quickly turned into tens of thousands. Tomorrow, Harish will go to Shree Ram Mandir and pray for a new year, a better beginning to the end he so desires. Kapila will accompany him, making sure to avoid the sweet sugar cubes that come in the prasad at the mandir, because she's diabetic. They will utter the same phrases their daughter and thousands more do tonight. They ask for sorrow to be removed from their minds and hearts, for happiness and wealth to come to their home, for pain to be wiped from their bodies.

Just three miles south, Sankumani and Shravani Sarma and their toddling son spend the day in prayer to the same goddess, whom they know as Durga, as she stands before a lion with one of her legs on the Mahishasura, or demon. The service they attend in a rented hall falls earlier in the day than the Navratri at Raritan Center and concludes well before Navratri's revelers even start dancing. Yet like Navratri, Durga Puja commemorates the conquest of demons. It is believed that Lord Rama, an incarnation of Vishnu, performed Durga Puja before he killed Ravana, an evil god, and then returned to his kingdom victorious. In Hindu texts, the battle of Rama and Ravana represents the eternal triumph of good over evil.

It is the Sarmas' second Durga Puja in America, and they continue to be struck by how much more religious, or at least ritual-observing, coming to America has made them. When they were teenagers in Assam, the northeastern province where both were born, Durga Puja meant days off from school, new clothes, big dinners, and trips around the city to view the re-creations of Durga's conquest. Displays competed with each other to attract the most attention. Like Navratri, they had been getting more commercial, satirical, even vulgar, and less religious. In the midst of the Clinton-Lewinsky scandal in 1998, for example, one tableau in Guwahati,

Assam's largest city, showed Monica Lewinsky as the goddess Durga and Bill Clinton as the evil she sought to slay.

In cosmopolitan Bombay, where the Sarmas last lived, they spent weeknights singing to each other as Sanku pumped the folds of a harmonium, an accordion-like instrument, with one hand and played its keys with the other. They spent weekends walking the city's beaches and bazaars. Yet they also dodged its traffic, beggars, and corruption. They left Bombay on March 3, 1999, software programmers riding the tech boom in the United States.

On the morning of Durga Puja, Sanku claims he isn't religious, never has been. "Yeah, then why do you pray every morning?" chides his wife, whose pet name of "Lipi" has stuck all these years. Sure enough, Sanku lights an incense stick after showering and recites the Gayatri Mantra before a small shrine the couple keeps in their kitchen.

Oh God! Thou art giver of life,
remover of pain and sorrow,
the provider of happiness.

Creator of the universe,
may we receive thy supreme
sin-destroying light.

May thou guide our intellect
in the right direction.

He says those words this morning, the morning he and his family commemorate Durga Puja. The actual holiday in India fell between September 28 and October 7, but as they do for so many festivals, Indians in America conveniently schedule the celebrations for Fridays, Saturdays, and Sundays.

As they ready themselves, Sanku's thoughts turn to two-year-old Chiku. "He's as good as back in Bombay or Delhi," he says. "He's exposed to more Assamese culture."

All their lives, Sanku and Lipi had been surrounded by Indians from all parts of India. Their best friends in Bombay had been from the southern state of Andhra Pradesh. Chiku's nanny was Marathi. Lipi's boss was from Jaipur. Upon immigrating to the United States, they suddenly found themselves mostly mixing with people from Assam and noticed that most Indians in America did the same. Gujaratis stuck with Gujaratis, Bengalis with Bengalis, Punjabis with the Punjabis.

On Oak Tree Road, of course, the groups mix as they shop and dine along the renowned shopping strip for South Asians. The cultural and commercial anchor sits in the midst of a bedroom community where there is no downtown; residents joke that's somewhere between the Menlo Park and Woodbridge Center malls. Yet weekends on Oak Tree Road—a strip situated partly in the Iselin hamlet of Woodbridge and partly in Edison—are alive, bustling, creating a carved-out downtown for New Jersey's Indian population. It's been called a range of names from "Little India" to "Little Calcutta" to "Bombay Boulevard." But everyone knows those names derisively come from old-time residents. The Indians simply call it Oak Tree Road.

In some ways, the commercial lane's existence allows the Sarmas to cling to their Indian roots more than ever. Whereas Lipi and Sanku once laughed at the predictable plots of Bollywood movies, lately they take them in on weekend nights, even buy the soundtracks to play in the car. They do their shopping in the Indian groceries, finding better okra and spinach leaves than in the supermarkets near their apartment.

On the morning they will perform Durga Puja, Sanku and Lipi have reason to be thankful. Both came to the United States on H-1B visas, awarded to highly specialized workers deemed to be in short supply among native Americans, Arguably, no other country reaped the benefits of the U.S. tech boom as did India, with its vast pool of English-speaking, highly educated labor. The H-1B visa allows holders to stay in the United States for six years—as long as they remain employed by the visa's sponsor. Just before Durga Puja, Congress passed a bill allowing the cap on the number of those visa holders to be raised from 115,000 to 195,000 per year for the next three years. Under the law, a U.S. employer would pay a $500 application fee for each worker sponsored on such a visa. Of those fees, more than half would go toward retraining American workers and another 15 percent would go toward programs to improve math and science education. Ironically, the money raised from the visas would be going to help ensure such visas would no longer need to be issued; Americans would be trained in the jobs now requiring imported labor.

Lipi and Sanku rejoice at another aspect of the new legislation. Namely, an H-1B holder will no longer be bound to a single employer in the process of getting a green card, the document that enables aliens to stay as long as they want and brands them permanent residents; the application can now move along with the worker to a new employer.

"No more slavery," Sanku says, only half joking.

From the kitchen, where she prepares lunch, Lipi chimes in. "The best thing for us is that we can change our employers while the green card is pending."

While Lipi and Sanku could have asked their employers to process their green cards right away, they decided to wait one year after their arrival. "Let's see if we like it," Lipi had said. In March 2000, they had gotten the lengthy procedure under way.

The Sarmas will attend Durga Puja with their friends—also from Assam, also on H-1B visas, Utpal and Malabika Brahma, who have come over for lunch. As they eat, the couples discuss the economy, news from home, and their families. Lipi's brother has just arrived in the United States and is attending college at Penn State. Malabika really enjoys being home with baby Disha. Soon, their talk turns to their role and fate in an economy that continues to sour. Recruiters don't call them as frequently as they once did. Could the tech boom really be waning?

"I just hope to keep my job," Utpal says to Sanku.

"Don't we all?" Sanku replies.

Both couples laugh as they feast on mushroom curry, fried eggplant, rice, and baked salmon. Hurriedly, Lipi puts the plates in the sink, fighting off Malabika's attempts to wash. "I'll do them later," she says. "We should go."

Durga Puja is being celebrated at rented-out halls and auditoriums across the state. The Sarmas and Brahmas choose the event at the Ukrainian Church and Cultural Center in nearby Somerset. There, two dozen Assamese, mostly arrivals to the United States within the last five years, meet them in a corner of the room they stake out. Most of the thousand or so people in the room are Bengalis, known for their ostentatious, colorful devotion to Ma Durga, an icon they decorate in flashy golds and deep reds.

As she approaches the group of familiar faces in the swarm of strangers, Malabika smiles, clutches Lipi's arm, and says, "I never did this as a schoolgirl, getting all dressed up and all. I really regret it."

Unlike the Navratri to be held later that night, where dancing and loud music mark the occasion, Durga Puja feels subdued. Aarti is done in the middle of the night at Navratri; during Durga Puja, the offering, known as anjali, comes before dinner. When the Sarmas and Brahmas arrive, anjali is just ending. Lipi goes over with Chiku in her arms to receive the blessing from the priest, or bahmun. He sprinkles flowers in their hair.

Om, Goddess Slayer of Demon Mahisa, Chanda, and Moonda.
The Great Illusionist, bestow unto me
Longevity, Restoration to Health and Victory.
Salutation to thee.

Om, Spouse of Lord Shiva, the cause and source of all
welfare, fulfiller of all ends. Om, Goddess

Uma, Spouse of Lord Brahama, celibacy in person, the body in which
the entire universe is
exhibited. Be pleased to me.

Om, Female leader of Gods, formidable, giver of progeny,
Amiable Eternity, ameliorator of
lineage, and fierce, Bestow me victory.
Salutation to thee.

After dinner, Sanku and Lipi don't bother staying for the cultural program, where there would be singing and dancing. As teenagers, this had always been their favorite part. Today, as parents, they can't stand to hear Chiku crying and screaming that he wants his favorite toy car, left at home. On the car ride home, Chiku falls asleep.

On the last day of Durga Puja as it is celebrated in India, the ornamented icons and the displays are carried through the streets and thrown into a nearby river. Some pieces sink; others float away. In New Jersey, festival and puja organizers store Amba and Durga and her various adornments in their closets and basements, only to be brought out again next year.

1

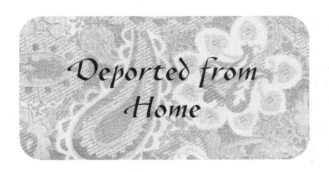

Deported from Home

Pradip Kothari arrived in November 1972, unimpressed with what he saw. He spent his first three months in Cleveland; the city's wet, dreary winter cast a gray spell over the shiny images Pradip had expected of America. Neon lights and signs seemed somehow dimmed by the season. Even guidebooks to the midwestern city warn its winters "can be a challenge to both the mental and physical health of any human person."

Pradip was spending those first months with his sister and her husband, both physicians, before starting a graduate program at Villanova University in suburban Philadelphia. He had no desire to be in the United States and went as far as to say he had been deported from his own home.

His parents felt differently. They told Pradip, then twenty-two, that they were shipping him off to learn responsibility. Pradip had served as general secretary of the student union at Maharajah Sayajirao University in Baroda, a school that was arguably the force behind that Gujarati city's cosmopolitan and cultural reputation. Protests and organizing were as much a part of Pradip's day as the kadhi, a Gujarati yogurt curry, and rice he ate at the end of his meal.

Before India marked its first quarter century of independence, Pradip's father, Ramanlal C. Kothari, pondered his family's future there. Ramanlal, the son of a village landowner and farmer, had seen firsthand the freedom an education could provide an Indian. He received his medical degree in the southern city of Madras, then returned to Baroda to marry in 1939 and establish an ophthalmology clinic. Both he and his wife followed the teachings of Mahatma Gandhi and were involved in the Congress Party, the party and leadership under which India gained independence in 1947. After meeting Gandhi in 1942, the Kotharis shed synthetic clothing and imports, embracing the homespun cotton, or khadi, that the pacifist advocated. Khadi allowed the Indians to boycott foreign goods while sending a message about their self-sufficiency. The Kotharis joined neighbors in burning clothes with foreign brand names, and soon Baroda's denizens, from beggars to bankers, were clothed in a sea of white saris, dhotis, and caps.

Ramanlal eventually prospered enough to buy an estate near Baroda's railroad station; with two stories, the house sprawled by Gujarati standards. He could afford to occasionally provide free eye surgery to the poor. He could afford tailored suits and crisp oxford shirts. Still, Ramanlal chose the homespun cotton and a white cap. More than symbols of struggle and pride, they served as tangible reminders of the principles of democracy and self-rule.

Then one day—sometime before Pradip left—Ramanlal no longer felt proud wearing the khadi.

Always a political symbol, khadi now shrouded politicians who had become corrupt leaders in Ramanlal's eyes. They pointed to their cloth as a symbol of their purity, but how could that be? To send your kids to Baroda's best schools meant paying a bribe. To pave the road in front of your home meant paying a bribe. Moreover, India's poor seemed as impoverished as ever.

"Show me any khadi man who's not exploiting others," Ramanlal demanded of contemporaries. They could only point to Ramanlal's wife, Sumati. "My people are not getting even clothes to hide their body," Ramanlal responded. That day, he gave up khadi.

Pradip, meanwhile, exhibited an exuberance and idealism Ramanlal knew all too well. Pradip had grown up with his parents backing a range of causes, from India's independence to the acceptance of lower castes, and followed their example in his college years. When he felt the professors in the chemical engineering department were poor teachers, Pradip led the students on a strike. When a crumbling wall facing the main road wasn't replaced, he circulated a petition. He tried to be a humanitarian activist as well. After the monsoon rains brought floods and left countless homeless, Pradip was sure to rush to the scene. Ramanlal feared his eldest son was becoming too obsessed with public work. Even more, he feared his son's efforts might be in vain.

Sumati, herself an activist for women's rights, lauded her son's inclination to work on behalf of causes, yet even she worried he'd never settle down into a career or family life if he stayed in Baroda. So it was decided Pradip would have to leave, whether he wanted to or not. His parents encouraged him to apply for graduate programs in computer science, viewing it as a stable field he could get a job in. Pradip, ever quick to protest, rally, advocate, remained the dutiful son and obeyed.

While Indian immigrants had arrived earlier in the century as laborers on the Transcontinental Railroad, the 1965 law opened America to highly educated professionals, such as doctors and engineers. It also served to widen the pool of international students in America, many of whom traced their roots to rural villages in India. In the late 1960s, many of those who had achieved success at boarding schools or colleges in India's cities applied for graduate study in the United States. Pradip, however, had been born and raised in Baroda and considered himself quite the city slicker. He arrived in America and found the city of Cleveland dreary and boring. Philadelphia, he would later recall, was not much better. In both places, Pradip was among a handful of Indians. If he faced any discrimination, it was not the overt kind he would recall years later.

In the summer of 1973, after a semester spent studying computer science, Pradip saw a U.S. economy in turmoil, mostly credited to the skyrocketing price of crude oil and the Arab oil embargo. In some ways, that year marked the end to decades of prosperity after World War II. Individual worker productivity, often used to measure standards of living, had grown nearly 3 percent a year in the postwar years. It fell to 1 percent after 1973.

Against this economic backdrop, Pradip's sister advised him to find a job quickly. She knew someone who worked in nuclear medicine, an imaging specialty that screens the body's organs and functions, and advised him to apply for a special course that provided three months of classes and nine months of training. Best of all, it provided a $350 monthly stipend.

Juggling the training in Philadelphia by day and courses at Villanova by night, Pradip lasted just one year and twenty-three credits at the university. The thought of more student loans and the lure of a steady paycheck led him to abandon school. In 1974, he took a job in nuclear medicine at Newark Beth Israel Hospital and moved to Elizabeth, New Jersey. It was on that job that he became known as "Peter," a name he doesn't recall giving himself. Two years later, his duty as a son called once again. His parents wanted him to marry.

Arranged marriages remain common throughout India, and Pradip's family had a long history of them. Still, his marriage to

Nandini in February 1976 was not exactly traditional. Pradip knew lots of women from his days in college, and lots of women knew him and his family. He endured several meetings with prospective brides during a trip to Baroda in December 1975. Like Gandhi, his family were followers of Vishnu and members of the Bania caste, which participated in business and government affairs in Gujarat. And like Gandhi, they professed not to care too much about caste.

Nandini Desai belonged to the highest caste; she was a Brahmin, although not an entirely pure one. Her maternal grandparents—a doctor and a nurse—had met on the job and fallen in love. He was a Brahmin, she a Parsi, an ethnic group that follows the monotheistic religion of Zoroastrianism. So even as a schoolgirl, Nandini knew that if she ever fell in love with someone and wanted to marry outside her caste, even her religion, her liberal family wouldn't necessarily disown her. She never did, though.

Nandini's father was keen for her to marry Pradip, despite his lower caste. Pradip's sister had married Nandini's cousin, so the two families were already bonded. *I've known him since my childhood,* Nandini thought. *There's no fear of what kind of guy he will be.* Admittedly, Pradip was considered a good match because he lived in America. At the time, Indians were starting to consider the United States a good place to go for a few years, earn a fortune, and then return to their motherland. Nandini's father wanted her to marry Pradip and move to the States so she could eventually sponsor her brother's and sister's immigration.

On February 18, 1976, Pradip and Nandini were wed in a ceremony attended by thousands of family and friends, including the maharaja and maharani of Baroda, who were frequent bridge partners of Pradip's parents. Pradip and Nandini exchanged garlands and took steps around a fire, then spent just a few days together as husband and wife before Pradip returned to the United States.

Not until five months later, in July, did Nandini secure her visa to join him. Unlike her new husband's, Nandini's first impressions of America were literally warm ones. Everything looked new and nice and sleek. The stores were different. In India, where separate stalls boasted milk, eggs, vegetables, sugar, butter, shopping had been an involved, lengthy process. It was a daylong affair against the backdrop of vendors' calls, the hissing of city buses, and the ringing of rickshaw bells and horns. Often, the merchants came to your home. Once you became a regular customer, they came at the same time every week. Supermarkets in America seemed much more convenient to Nandini, although with all the brands and varieties, she often felt as if she could stay there all day, too.

They lived in a basement apartment in Elizabeth, a fading industrial city increasingly becoming home to minorities and immigrants. Nandini liked it well enough but started to get bored quickly. The apartment had just one bedroom. It didn't take that long to clean. Cooking for just the two of them didn't take long either. Nandini wondered how far her bachelor's degree in home science and library science would take her.

To ease her boredom, Nandini started volunteering at the hospital Pradip worked in, Newark Beth Israel. After a month, the medical records division asked her to fill in for someone for a week. When they asked her to stay, she did.

Four years passed. Pradip honored his parents' wish that he become a family man. Nandini immersed herself in her work, making friends quickly with the other women, who loved to go out to lunch or bake cakes to celebrate the smallest milestones. On June 20, 1980, Nandini gave birth to a baby girl, Payal. She took six months off before she returned to work, leaving Payal in the care of an Indian nanny.

According to the census taken the year of Payal's birth, the Kotharis were among 400,000 Indians living in the United States, 19,500 of them in New Jersey. But in the years following, many more immigrants started to join the Kotharis and head to New Jersey. Some couldn't afford city rents anymore, dubbed "strangling" by a *New York Times* real estate columnist that year. A one-bedroom with seven hundred square feet—luxurious by city standards—in a new building was more than $1,000 per month. In the early 1980s, the vacancy rate in Manhattan was less than 1 percent. Still others were lured to suburbs by the prospect of home ownership and good schools. Their migration started in northern New Jersey, in outer cities like Jersey City, Union City, and Elizabeth. Eventually, they started to trickle south.

It's easy to see why. Middlesex County sits at the crossroads of the New Jersey Turnpike, the Garden State Parkway and U.S. Route 1. New Jersey Transit's Northeast Corridor line runs through New Brunswick, Edison, Metuchen, and Metro Park, so commuters reach offices within New York City skyscrapers in under an hour. Philadelphia is just over an hour away. "The widest cultural divide was between those who said stoop, lightning bug, and sub (New York) and those who said porch, firefly, and hoagie (Philadelphia)," proclaimed a *New York Times* article on the area.

Through the 1980s, the county's population increased by 76,000 people, a growth partially fueled by Asian and Latino immigrants. Meanwhile, Edison grew by 18,000 people to a population of 89,000; half the newcomers were Asian. Over the decade, township libraries started to offer English classes for new arrivals from India, China, Korea, the Philippines, Hungary, and Poland. By the end of the 1980s, the county college would have increased the number of its English classes for newcomers from ten to a whopping seventy-five.

Pradip, seeing a business opportunity in the burgeoning immigrant group, started a travel agency as a side business. It was an industry he was familiar with. In the late 1960s, before immigrating, he had helped a family friend set up his travel agency in Baroda, then Surat, another Gujarati city. For years, his friend had tried to get Pradip to start a U.S. operation. Finally, Pradip relented, but selling only to friends and family. Tickets to India were much cheaper from a consolidator, someone willing to buy multiple bookings directly from the airline and then sell them to passengers.

By 1983, the Kotharis had saved enough to buy a house in the Avenel section of Woodbridge, where tracts of land were quickly being replaced with leafy neighborhoods. By then, Pradip's travel business was booming, Nandini was working full time at the hospital, and Payal had entered daycare. Much to the chagrin of its residents, Avenel is perhaps best known as the location of a correctional facility for sex offenders. Compared to neighboring Colonia, it is considered more working class. But it was just fine for the Kotharis, especially since buying in Avenel enabled them to move into a brand-new home. Their split-level three-bedroom house sat on tree-lined Borman Avenue, where basketball hoops and station wagons filled driveways.

On January 28, 1983, Toral was born. Again, Nandini took six months off and then returned to work.

That year, Pradip expanded his travel agency into a full-time operation and opened an office near his home. He named it Quick Travel, the same as his friend's business in Gujarat.

With New Jersey's Indian population exploding, tickets to their homeland were always in demand. The airlines warned him that the hub of travel, especially for overseas, was in New York, not New Jersey. Seeing the growth of the Indian community around him, though, Pradip decided to risk it. He had had dreams of seeing the world for free while his employees fielded reservations. Quickly, Pradip learned that small business owners rarely get to leave.

Indians who immigrated in the 1970s tended to favor professional jobs, likely a holdover from the British colonial tradition of civil service—the ultimate source of job stability. By one estimate, just 14 percent of Indians owned their own business, compared to 33 percent of Korean immigrants. Going into business for himself, Pradip was joining a new breed of Indian immigrant: the self-employed.

Between 1982 and 1987, the number of Indian-owned businesses increased 120 percent to nearly 30,000, according to the Census Bureau. Some owners were like Pradip, older immigrants who had saved enough capital to venture into entrepreneurship. Others represented a new wave of Indians seeking refuge in the United States: Indians from Africa. They had once been traders or owners of small stores; in America, they discovered opportunities taking over small motels, gas stations, and convenience stores. By 1994, more than 7,200 Indian owners operated 12,500 of the country's 28,000 budget hotels and motels, according to the Atlanta-based Asian-American Hotel Owners Association. This phenomenon was the backdrop to Mira Nair's movie *Mississippi Masala*, in which an Indian family is expelled from Uganda when Idi Amin takes power. The family runs a motel in Mississippi and the Indian daughter falls in love with a black man, much to her father's dismay. Soon so many motels were being run by Gujaratis who had immigrated to the United States, many via Africa or the United Kingdom, that Indian-operated motels came to be known as "Patel motels" after Gujarat's most popular surname. (The name has its roots in ancient India, where rulers appointed a record keeper to track annual crops on each parcel of land, or "pat." That person became known as a "patel.")

Gujaratis' success in the United States can be chalked up to several factors. Their home, historically a province of strategic ports and commerce and trade, ranks among India's more prosperous states. But experts say Gujaratis rely on family connections more than other Indian subgroups. "There can never be just one successful Patel because he'll always share his good fortune with other Patels," Lavina Melwani writes in an issue of *Little India* magazine illustrating its cover story on Gujaratis with an ethnic-motif pot sitting atop mounds of U.S. dollar bills.

In 1986, as immigration laws changed to allow immigrants to sponsor relatives, Pradip and Nandini sent for the remaining members of their family. Ramanlal and Sumati, Pradip's parents, visited frequently but refused to stay for long. They had their own projects in Baroda. Ramanlal was helping run a free medical clinic. Sumati worked as a social worker in a women's center where women learned skills from book-binding to reading to sewing.

The communities surrounding the Kotharis started to reflect the population shifts of the 1980s. Along the section of U.S. Route 1 that ran through the county, truck stops were being replaced with restaurants, cottage-style motels with luxury hotels, a Montgomery Ward warehouse with a doctor's clinic. "Highways are really becoming the showcases of their community," a Piscataway commercial real estate broker told the *News Tribune* in 1986. "The Edison area is changing very rapidly and all the better. We're giving a new image to the town."

Houses in Edison for under six figures were suddenly unheard of. That same year, a real estate agent on Oak Tree Road lamented to the local paper that it seemed only the affluent had a chance at home ownership in central Jersey. "There are some places in South Edison that can go for a little bit lower, but they're all slab homes, no basement," she said. "If you're not qualified, you're not going to buy into North Edison."

Middlesex County was going upscale.

Indeed, change abounded throughout the region. Along a strip in the Iselin section of Woodbridge known as Oak Tree Road, a handful of Indian entrepreneurs set up shop. In 1986, the Ashoka restaurant opened. Then came Nina Jewelers and Sona Jewelers. Chowpatty, an Indian restaurant named after a famous beach, followed.

As a businessman catering to Indian immigrants, Pradip eyed the changes with interest. *Oak Tree Road is a decrepit strip,* he thought. *So few businesses operate there anymore. Ethnic enclaves and commercial markets are a purely urban phenomenon. We Indians already have Jackson Heights in the city. Will these Indian businesses survive here?*

The area's reception of the Indian businesses could be characterized as cool at best. The day after Jaswant Singh, owner of Ashoka, put up the Grand Opening sign on the Indian restaurant in 1986, he arrived to find his decorations destroyed and the entrance defaced. Other shopkeepers reported taunting, eggs thrown at their windows, and strained relations with neighbors. Rarely did they report anything to police.

Pradip simply observed. Nearly fifteen years before, he had made a promise to his parents to stay out of politics. Besides, he was busy with his fledgling business and increased household duties. Nandini had shifted her hours so she could leave in the early morning. Pradip now struggled to get breakfast on the table, rubber bands around his daughters' thick black curls, and the pair out the door before they missed their bus. Then he'd go to work, and Nandini would be home in time to give the girls an after-school snack. His wife and daughters were usually asleep by the time Pradip returned home from the travel agency. The Kothari home became like so many in America, harried and hectic, headed by two working parents.

Nonetheless, Pradip watched the growing resentment toward Indians closely. Even closer, he watched what was happening farther north. With only a narrow river separating it from New York, Jersey City had become home to more than 10,000 Indians. The more that arrived, the more self-sustaining their community became, united by religion, food, and customs. "We don't get into crime. Our children are getting top awards at schools. What more could you ask from a community?" said Lalitha Masson, a doctor who moved to Jersey City Heights in 1966. "The hospitals in this city were abandoned by white doctors. So for many years they were run by Pakistani and Indian doctors."

The result was success. The result was a quick realization of the American Dream. The result was also jealousy. "I been in this country all my life and they come in and plop down $200,000 for a house," one longtime Jersey City resident told a reporter.

Tensions simmering, on August 7, 1987, the *Jersey Journal* received an anonymous letter. "We will go to any extreme to get the Indians to move out of Jersey City," it said in an uneven scrawl. "WE ARE FOR REAL. We will be taken seriously. Patels will LEAVE." There was no signature, just a slash drawn through a dot. The newspaper called the FBI and did not publish the letter.

On August 8, the next day, as a man named Bharat Kanu-Bhai Patel slept in his Jersey City apartment, two men later identified to be James Kerwin and Peter Jester broke in and beat him with a metal pipe, injuring his arms and back. Patel's only crime: he was listed in the phone book. Apparently, Kerwin and Jester had thumbed through the telephone directory, turned to the list of Patels, and settled on Bharat Patel as their victim. Neighbors described Kerwin and Jester as nice boys from good families in Jersey City Heights, a middle-class section of the city that had always been solidly Irish and Italian. Nice boys who didn't like their new neighbors.

They called themselves the "Dotbusters." The name referred to the red dot Indian women often wear in the center of their foreheads as a decoration. Many news accounts of the time referred to the dot, or bindi, as a sign of marriage, but bindis are worn by the married and unmarried alike. They come in all shapes and sizes and colors, often chosen to match the colors of a woman's sari or salwar kameez, a loose tunic worn over drawstring pants.

In the late hours of September 24, 1987, as an Indian doctor, Khaushal Sharan, left a downtown Jersey City office building and passed a firehouse, a band of three men yelled, "There's a dothead. Let's get him." Sharan was beaten with a baseball bat so severely that he spent a week in a coma. He left the hospital after three weeks with permanent neurological damage—and no recollection of the events.

The three alleged attackers were acquitted. Years later, as a judge reviewed the investigation that had been conducted into the beating, he chastised police for not interviewing the officers who responded to the scene, the thirty or forty youth who gathered to watch, or the firefighters on duty that night in the firehouse. "If this had been a policeman who was beaten up and left in front of the firehouse, we know what kind of investigation would have taken place," said Judge Joseph E. Irenas of the federal district court in Camden.

The day after the doctor's beating, the *Jersey Journal* published the letter it had received with a story about bias crime throughout the state. Two days later, a Friday night, Navrose Mody, a thirty-year-old manager at Citibank, was walking home to Jersey City Heights with a white colleague when he was cornered outside a bar in Hoboken by four teenagers. They started to call Mody, left hairless at an early age by a genetic defect, "baldy," "Kojak," and "glowhead."

"Leave us alone. Stop playing. We're not kids," Mody responded.

A girl ran after him, told by the others to slap him on the head. Mody turned around and pushed her in the chest area. Lawyers for the teens would later say that Mody grabbed her breasts and that the male teens fought out of a sense of chivalry. They knocked Mody's colleague unconscious, then turned on Mody.

Mody assumed a defensive position learned in karate, but the four youth proved too strong for him. He was knocked down and hit his head on a fire hydrant. He got up. He was knocked down again onto the hydrant. He got up. He was knocked down again, this time onto the curb. He lay there, bleeding.

Mody suffered severe head trauma and slipped into a coma. He died three days later.

Authorities said the teens had no connection to the Dotbusters and that they taunted Mody because he was bald. His father and family lawyer maintained the incident was racially motivated. "I haven't heard of Telly Savalas being attacked on his frequent jaunts to Atlantic City," said lawyer Marc Bernstein, referring to the actor who played Kojak on the television series.

The two violent attacks came amid a series of incidents targeting Indians in northern New Jersey. "Hindus Go Home" was spray-painted on the lobby wall of an apartment building on Central Avenue, the strip where many of Jersey City's Indian stores sit. An Indian family rang in 1988 with a letter bomb, discovered on New Year's Day. On March 11 of that year, another Indian family in Jersey City reported obscenities scrawled on the wall of their home.

Still, police did not treat the incidents as a wave of bias crimes. In the spring of 1988, Precinct Captain James Galvin, whose office was steps away from the Indian-owned stores on Central Avenue, characterized Indians' growing protests as "95 percent overreacting. They get a snowball through the window and they want a car there right away." He admitted that the Indian immigrants and the white residents didn't really understand each other. "It's like the blacks in the '60s."

Yet the comparison was not quite valid, for it was clear the attacks were motivated by more than racism. There was resentment of the success Indian immigrants appeared to have achieved so quickly. There was a message being sent that they didn't belong. Indians took to the streets in protest, one of the first public displays of activism the community showed.

The assaults mobilized the Indian community but also taught the immigrants a stark lesson about the realities of discrimination in America. And in some ways, the violence worked. Indian women packed away saris and bought blouses and blue jeans. They no longer circled red bindis from canisters of vermilion powder onto their foreheads each morning. They made their children stay indoors after dark. Some put their homes and apartments up for sale and sought refuge in suburbs with growing Indian populations, such as Middlesex County.

It would only be a temporary escape, as the violence soon followed Indians south.

In the late 1980s, Indian immigrants' mark on Edison and surrounding areas became much more visible. The township's high schools—J. P. Stevens and Edison High—started to graduate valedictorians named Patel and Shah and Gupta. School officials often take credit for the Indian migration, saying Indians were drawn to good schools. Others say involved, often obsessive, Indian parents helped turn the schools around.

Still, tensions continued to simmer. There had been signs of it before, when Jaswant Singh opened his store or Chandrakant Patel found egg on the windows of Chowpatty. But as Oak Tree Road started to attract more Indian businesses, their more-established neighbors wondered if there was still room for them.

Pradip kept his promise to his parents. Through the late 1980s, he eyed what was going on in Jersey City angrily—but stayed out of it. Early in 1990, his travel agency's lease about to expire, Pradip discovered a space for rent on Oak Tree Road. First a post office, then an insurance agency, it had sat empty for eighteen months, Pradip decided it was time his business catering to the Indian community sat among other Indian merchants. So far, he'd been able to prove the airlines' prediction wrong, but his business could only grow if he moved it to an area where Indians could buy their spices and saris as they waited for passport photos and tickets.

In May 1990, Pradip relocated Quick Travel to Oak Tree Road. On the first official day of business, he reported to work to find his windows smashed; rocks and bottles were scattered in the front waiting room. He called police. They told him to call the insurance company.

Then and there, Pradip abandoned the promise he'd made to Ramanlal and Sumati nearly two decades ago. He could no longer remain silent.

2

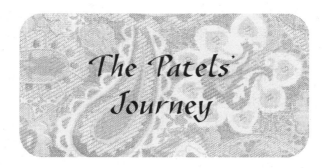

The Patels' Journey

Harish Patel's eyes fixed on the door exiting customs at John F. Kennedy International Airport. For almost two years, the forty-three-year-old had started his day at 8:00 A.M. as a factory worker and ended it at midnight as a security guard to earn and save enough money for his wife and two daughters to join him. Their arrival would make the family whole again, Harish thought. And what a day they had picked to begin life in America. It was July 3, 1990. His daughters would surely find the next day's fireworks display near Harish's apartment in Edison reminiscent of those put on for their new year of Diwali.

Harish looked up when he heard the automatic doors open. Indians, some clad in saris, others in jeans and T-shirts, started to exit. Finally, Harish caught sight of his wife, Kapila, pushing a cart of suitcases, hand luggage, and shopping bags. She was wearing a salwar kameez. Behind her came the girls, Zankhana and Kajal, ages fifteen and eight.

Harish went to them and touched Kapila's arm. He patted Kajal on the head and assessed how much she had grown. Addressing her with the Gujarati word for daughter, he said: "Beti, do you remember me?"

Kajal looked up at Harish. "No," she said. "I don't."

He couldn't blame her. Since Kajal was a toddler, Harish had been flying back and forth between the United States and India. He had lived in Detroit; Durham, North Carolina; Hollywood, California; Lowell, Massachusetts; and three places in New Jersey—Jersey City, the Fords section of Woodbridge, and finally Edison. None had ever felt like home. In Harish's mind, home would only be one place: his simple two-bedroom house near close friends and extended family in Baroda. Back home, Harish Patel had worked as a supervisor in the foreign-exchange division of the Bank of Baroda. He started in 1970 as a teller, earning 250 rupees per month, and worked his way up to management. As a manager, he was able to sign cash-withdrawal forms and those who reported to him called him "sir." When Harish left the bank for good, his salary was 5,500 rupees a month, at the time more than most Indians made in a year.

Among his jobs in the United States, he pumped gas, packed boxes, filled pill bottles rolling off an assembly line, watched for shoplifters as a security guard, and sold newspapers. His two brothers who had preceded him to the States never told him of the hardship that came with living in there. Instead, their stories of America—the cars, the jeans, the money—impressed Harish Patel enough to lure him away from home. Since then, Harish had spent every day in America convincing himself the greater opportunity, especially the chance for his daughters to get a good education, was worth turning his back on home.

Harish Patel was born the same year that India won its independence from the British, 1947. He benefited from one of the remnants of British colonial rule, namely, an English education. When Harish was a boy, his parents were among the millions of

Indians who left their villages for opportunities in the city. The grandsons of a bullock farmer and sons of a civil engineer, Harish and his four brothers were taught to value education and professional types of work. He became a banker after earning his bachelor's degree in economics from the University of Ahmedabad, a city about 110 miles from Baroda. On May 21, 1970, at the age of twenty-three, he wed Kapila, then eighteen, in a marriage arranged one month before. In the 1970s, two of Harish's brothers emigrated from Gujarat to the United States. One found work as a civil engineer in Detroit; the other was admitted to Duke University in Durham, North Carolina, for a Ph.D. program. The brothers returned to India every three or four years; each time, they bestowed gifts of dolls and dresses upon Harish's daughters and impressed everyone with the value of their dollar once converted to the Indian rupee. *American money can be spent like water,* Harish observed.

His elder daughter, Zankhana, wanted her father to be a part of that lifestyle. "Papa, why don't you go to America?" she repeatedly asked. Harish saw no reason not to try, so he agreed to allow his eldest brother, Arvind, to sponsor him on an immigration status that would eventually lead to a green card.

On March 20, 1985, carrying a one-way ticket and $20, Harish landed in America. He arrived in a nation whose dollar was steadily falling; on the day Harish's plane touched down, newspapers nationwide reported that consumer confidence suffered the worst drop in twenty years after the closure of seventy private savings and loan institutions.

Harish flew to Detroit to join Arvind, a civil engineer. For a week, Harish tried to find work, searching through classified ads every morning. He soon gave up and asked Arvind to lend him money to return home, since he was officially on a leave from his banking job. His brother refused and resorted to tough love: "If you want to go back, you'll have to get a job and make the money on your own."

Harish then went to Durham to stay with his younger brother Indravadan, who helped him find a maintenance job at a restaurant, collecting trash, sweeping the sidewalks, and watering the landscaping for $3.25 per hour. After four days of performing work Harish felt was beneath him, he decided to try his luck in New York City at the urging of family friends who lived in Queens. Two weeks of searching for a job produced nothing, so he called an old friend of his father's in Jersey City who owned a candy store. The storeowner agreed to pay Harish $3 per hour as a guard. Harish was specifically told to "watch the black people who try to steal." That job ended when Harish started to fear the people he was told to watch and reprimand. Harish recalled what he had heard about black people in India. "Negroes shoot at sight," a classmate once told him. At about five-foot-seven and 180 pounds, Harish is not a slight man, but he thought no amount of weight could save him from the guns the storeowner told him thieves and shoplifters carried.

Already in debt to his brothers and the family friends who had been housing him and giving him pocket money, Harish panicked at the thought of spending any more time in the United States. He stopped smoking cigarettes because he could no longer afford them. Finally, Harish landed a job at an Emerson Radio warehouse in North Bergen, New Jersey, as a material handler. For $4.25 per hour, he took television sets off the assembly line and loaded them into boxes lined with Styrofoam. For four months, he worked ten-hour days, taking hot baths in his friend's Jersey City apartment to soothe his aching back.

With each paycheck, Harish counted down from $600, the price of an airline ticket. By October, he had saved $457. Harish couldn't wait any longer to get home. He called his brother in North Carolina and successfully begged for $150 so he could buy a ticket to Bombay. Just before he left, Harish Patel received his green card, ensuring he could return to the United States as one of its permanent residents.

Harish slipped back into his old job at the Bank of Baroda. He resumed smoking. Unlike his brothers, who raved about America's virtues upon their returns to India, Harish reported to everyone he met that America was an awful, lonely, backbreaking place to live and work. "Don't go, don't go," he told whomever he could.

Still, in May 1987, when a friend called him and told him he could use some help running his motel in Hollywood, California, Harish returned. Here was a chance to try America again with a job in hand. Besides, Harish reasoned, he had to return to America within two years after his green card was issued or face its revocation. Harish once again found a weakening U.S. economy. Inflation and gas prices were up, stock markets volatile.

The motel was in a section of town with a lot of blacks, Harish said, and he was scared once again. When he overheard his friend's wife complaining about Harish living in the motel for free, Harish knew it was time to return to Gujarat. He had not lasted in America even twenty-five days.

He did not last in Baroda for much longer. In the fall of 1988, Harish couldn't ignore the differences between India and America anymore. In India, government officials were corrupt and accepted, even demanded, bribes for routine services. Luckily, Zankhana and Kajal were able to attend the school of their choice without the Patels having to pay a bribe, but Harish heard from neighbors and relatives that such bribes were becoming the norm. *How long can my family last in India?* Harish vowed to try America once more, despite now familiar reports of its economy softening. Once again, Harish returned to the United States, this time to Lowell, Massachusetts, to stay with a distant relative of his in-laws.

Sajjan Bhagat knew of Harish's futility and frustration in the United States and vowed things would be different this time. As soon as Harish awoke the morning after his arrival, Sajjan took him to a job he had already found for his friend as a security guard in an office complex. To pay off the money Harish had borrowed from his brothers and friends, he worked sixteen-hour days from 4:00 P.M. until 8:00 A.M. Sajjan taught him how to drive; Harish obtained his driver's license and bought a used car. He found himself happy for the first time in America. But after five months, Harish received a phone call from his younger brother. "Harish, you're a banker," Jyotindra said. "Why are you working as a security guard?" Ashamed, Harish said he would move south for better opportunities.

Harish sold his car, returned to New Jersey, and moved into an apartment in Jersey City with his brother. He quickly found work on a pharmaceutical company's assembly line. For his job readying bottles of ibuprofen for shipping, Harish stuck the label on the bottle, waited for one hundred capsules to be dropped into its open mouth—he had to count them himself—and capped the bottle before the next filling, seconds later. Sometimes, if he was too slow or the machine too fast, the pills would spill across the counter and Harish would have to start the count to one hundred all over again. To Harish, the job didn't feel like a step up from a security guard. So after three months, when his supervisor at the Bank of Baroda sent word that he had to return or face termination, Harish happily went home.

By the winter of 1988, Harish had been back and forth between the United States and Baroda three times in as many years. That winter, the New Jersey Senate passed a $16.5 million aid package to help the state's thousands of unemployed residents. New Jersey governor Tom Kean imposed a hiring freeze. AT&T laid off 16,000 workers. Yet an ocean away in India, Harish's daughter Zankhana, then thirteen, couldn't understand why he wasn't making it like her uncles had. "You're just not trying hard enough, Papa," she said. "Next time when you go, you can't come back. We'll come to you."

Harish didn't bother explaining to her that he had been competing with thousands of the native-born unemployed for work or that banks had already told him he had little chance succeeding in

America. "Your systems in India are different from ours," they would say. They were right. In Indian banks, each teller was given a different task, authorizing withdrawals or deposits or check cashing, but never all at the same time. It would be more than a decade until most Indian banks were computerized; instead, each account number and signature had to be authorized from a registry of books kept in stacks behind the tellers' desks. The first computers Harish ever saw were in America. Not only did the Indian system employ workers who never learned all aspects of running a bank, but it also made for long lines and impatient customers. Even as the twenty-first century began, the Bank of Baroda's main room remained separated into lines under signs that said Remittances, Saving Bank Accounts, Current Accounts, Overdrafts, Cash Receipts, Cash Payments. Harish was almost tempted to agree with the banks that told him he had no chance, except that he felt most comfortable and respectable as a banker. Those other jobs would be just something he'd endure until the right opportunity came along.

Harish thought about trying to get white-collar work in clerical, bookkeeping, or accounting positions, but those jobs seemed to require English skills he didn't have. His English was perfectly understandable, but when interviewers started talking fast, he tended to get easily confused and lost in the conversation. If he didn't understand a concept, he pretended not to understand the English. For years after immigrating, Harish could not conduct an extensive phone conversation in English. He did not tell his daughters and Kapila, who were living off the family's savings, that employers told him he was "hard to understand" or had "too heavy an accent."

In the spring of 1989, Harish Patel returned to the United States with his daughter's words echoing throughout the eighteen-hour plane ride between Bombay and JFK International. This time, he moved in as a paying guest with his brother and sister-in-law in Woodbridge and found work nearby at an Exxon gas station.

He paid $150 per month to sleep on his brother's couch. One morning, he awoke to hear the couple fighting. "How long is he going to stay?" his sister-in-law demanded of his brother. "How long is this going to go on?"

Harish didn't hear his brother's response, but soon thereafter his brother asked for $200 monthly instead. Harish paid him the money right away and said he would find another place to live.

When his boss at the gas station, a turbaned Sikh man named Inderpal Singh, heard of Harish's situation, he said, "You can come live with my people." Harish, who had lived only with Gujaratis until now, was unsure. In India, many Hindus have an unfavorable image of Sikhs. Jokes about sardars, the Hindi term for turbaned men, abound in India similar to Polish jokes in the United States. Harish had heard all the stereotypes but had no alternative. He moved into a one-bedroom apartment with three Sikhs. The four men took turns cooking, but Harish, a devout Hindu who rarely ate meat, could not eat the dishes the others prepared. He was also hopeless in the kitchen. One of the roommates, Bira Singh, took a liking to Harish and specially prepared rotis, flattened wheat-flour bread, and daal, a lentil dish, for him to eat every night. *Such a friendship would have been rare in Gujarat,* Harish thought.

Harish obtained a second job in the shipping department of Revlon, packing boxes of makeup and hair-care products. Between a ten-hour-per-day stint at Revlon and a four-hour shift at the Exxon station, he saved $8,000 over five months. For those five months, his lone expense was $250 monthly for room and board. He wore old clothes, spotted in gasoline grease that no washing machine could erase. He did not buy a single cigarette for five months. His savings were just enough to bring the rest of his family over and make a deposit on an apartment rental of his very own. Still, signs of a sluggish U.S. economy abounded, and economists debated whether the nation was already in a recession.

On the day she arrived in America, Zankhana Patel sat in the backseat as her father drove from the airport down the New Jersey Turnpike in a car borrowed from Bira Singh. She had never seen her father drive before. Back at home in Baroda, her family, like most others, traveled by buses, taxis, or auto- and bicycle-rickshaws. Already, Zankhana thought, America was looking beautiful. The stores they passed in the airport were so sleek and shiny. She had heard all about the way America would be from her uncles and cousins; they raved about the opportunities that abounded in the States, but Zankhana had always been a person who needed to see it to believe it. Granted, her father complained of how hard life was, but Zankhana thought he just wasn't ready to give America a chance. And even though he complained of being poor, he had always brought home toys, games, jewelry, and clothing for her and Kajal. The clothes from America just *felt* different. Zankhana spent most of her life wearing loose salwar kameezes, but she loved the skirts and tops her father would bring for her so much more. So how bad could America be? Maybe now that she, Kajal, and Ma were joining him, things would be more stable.

Within an hour, the Patels reached their new home in the Hilltop Estates apartment complex in Edison. For $600 per month, Harish was renting a one-bedroom apartment; he had borrowed the $1,200 deposit from Inderpal Singh, the gas-station owner, The arrangement was to be temporary; as soon as they had more money, the family could move to a two-bedroom. Harish selected Hilltop because it was less than a mile from the Indian groceries and restaurants on Oak Tree Road in neighboring Woodbridge. He also knew that many of the families in Hilltop spoke Gujarati, so his wife's and daughters' acclimation would be easier.

Hilltop Estates was built in the 1960s to accommodate a population burgeoning thanks to the baby boom and the growth of assembly plants and office parks in the area. Hilltop had always been a magnet for immigrant groups, including refugees housed in nearby Camp Kilmer after escaping the Hungarian Revolution in 1956. In the 1960s, many of these Hungarians opted to stay in central New Jersey and found employment at New Brunswick–based Johnson & Johnson and at companies in the Raritan Center industrial park. In the 1970s, Vietnamese and Korean immigrants dominated Hilltop; they were replaced by Indians—mostly Gujaratis and Punjabis—in the 1980s and 1990s. The shabby-looking apartment complex has been home to thousands of arrivals straight from Newark and JFK airports (that most immigrants now disembark off planes makes the FOB label an obvious misnomer). For immigrants in Edison, Hilltop has historically been the step before home ownership. The lucky ones, anyway.

Dusk fell as the Patels, toting their luggage, slowly climbed one flight of stairs to the second floor of a brown wooden building. It resembled all the others around it except for the yellow numbers labeling it 29. Harish opened the door to the apartment, which the family discovered empty except for two pillows and a piece of carpet in the living room. It took Zankhana and Kajal all of a minute to walk around.

Harish Patel had warned his family to expect meager beginnings. Zankhana thought Hilltop wasn't so bad—to her, it looked like any other apartment complex. She was more upset that her father hadn't thought to buy any furniture. Still, she was certain the situation would be temporary and they would be living more luxuriously soon.

Knowing her husband's ineptitude at cooking, Kapila had packed most of her supplies and spices from her kitchen in her suitcases and gotten them through customs. Upon inspecting her new kitchen, she discovered Harish had thought ahead enough to buy rice and daal. Kapila began to cook dinner for her family, using ingredients from both her old and new homes.

Over dinner, eaten sitting cross-legged on the living room floor as they did in Gujarat, Harish started to tell his family stories of his life in America thus far. None was a very happy tale, and all involved high hopes and repeated failure. He told them he had wanted them to come on July 3 because the next day was Independence Day and that meant he wouldn't have to lose a vacation day. Vacation days were hard to come by, he said. "And nobody's going to help you in this country," he told his daughters. "You have to do it on your own."

That night, the family slept on the same floor where they'd eaten. The next day's Fourth of July fireworks went unwitnessed by the nation's newcomers as they slept off the long journey and jet lag.

In September 1990, on Kajal's first day at the Menlo Park Primary School, she refused to talk to any of the other fourth graders. She had spent the summer at home as much as possible, despite her father's insistence that she talk to shop clerks to practice English. Now, two months after she moved to America, Kajal still refused to answer the phone in her own home. She had tried to say something in school that morning and a classmate didn't understand her English. She was in regular classes for most of the day with one afternoon English-as-a-second-language course. Kajal kept her head looking down toward her notebook. She had styled her hair in a short boy cut. All the kids were looking at her funny as if they couldn't tell if she was a boy or a girl.

When the teacher called on her, Kajal stood, as she had been expected to do in India to show respect for the teacher. The class giggled. "KAY-jal," the teacher said, pronouncing it the way Kajal would soon say her own name, "in this country, you do not need to stand when addressed." Kajal sat down and vowed to remain silent forever.

The teasing about her accent persisted over the next few days, despite the fact that many of Kajal's classmates were also Indians, even fellow Gujaratis. The schoolwork was different and more difficult than back in Baroda. Less than a month into the academic year, Kajal refused to attend school. Harish took three days off his two jobs. On the first day, he offered his young daughter lecture after lecture on how important education was, how without it Kajal would be doomed to mediocrity, how he had left his homeland for her education, her future, the family's better life. On the next two days, Harish—who had bought a second-hand car over the summer—drove Kajal to and from school, dropping her off at her classroom and picking her up when the school day was over. She didn't miss school anymore, although she still tried to remain silent whenever possible.

Meanwhile, at J. P. Stevens High School, Zankhana was ecstatic to be placed in eleventh grade. In Baroda, she had finished Class 10, a standard equivalent to high school graduation that is often followed by two years of preuniversity. But her concentration had been Gujarati, not a subject she would be able to pick up at Stevens. After taking the math and writing tests at the high school, Zankhana feared she would need to repeat a grade or, worse, take remedial classes. Her results, however, placed her in regular classes in the eleventh grade. Unlike Kajal's, Zankhana's first year in American school included fast friendships with other recently arrived immigrants and American-born Indians. With a fair complexion and long black hair resembling that of a Bollywood actress, Zankhana was also admired by many of the Hilltop Gang, a group of high school– and college-age men from the apartment complex. Zankhana's father disapproved of her hanging out with boys too much, though, so she rarely told him when she did. Expected to be home by 9:00 P.M., Zankhana, who frequently tried her parents' patience, didn't test her father on that issue. She feared his temper because it brought out hers.

Soon, Zankhana started to feel suffocated by her parents and desired more freedom. If she couldn't go out with friends after 9:00, she could work, couldn't she? Zankhana decided she would get a job and offer most of her earnings to her parents. Her father encouraged this, not only because money was tight at home but also so she could practice her English skills. Kapila decided she, too, could work on weekends and while the girls were in school, so the two went off in search of work together. They found jobs as clerks at Shopper's World, a discount department store in South Plainfield. Zankhana worked there for most of her junior year, spending 7:00 A.M. until 3:00 P.M. at school and 4:00 P.M. until 10:00 P.M. at work. Homework took a backseat to making money.

Over the next two years, the family settled into life in America and their apartment, buying secondhand furniture and befriending neighbors. Zankhana switched jobs every few months, working at Kentucky Fried Chicken, Kmart, and Bradlees, among others. Her stint at Burger King was a short-lived one. As a vegetarian, Zankhana only handled meat if it was on a tray or in a takeout bag. One day, during an understaffed shift, her manager asked her to separate the beef patties and place them on the grill.

"Forget it. I'm not going to do that," Zankhana said. "I'd rather do dishes all day."

"You either separate the meat or go home."

Zankhana went home and found another job the next day.

Zankhana relied on her father and co-worker for rides, often returning as late as midnight. She and Kapila took their road tests for their driver's licenses. Zankhana passed. Kapila failed parallel parking and was afraid to try again.

During the summer of 1991, as the economy continued to slump, Harish lost his $5.50-per-hour job at the factory. His inclination to move during tough times took the family to Philadelphia. A friend had told him the rent there was cheaper. It was. The family found a two-bedroom apartment across from the Franklin Mills Mall for $365 monthly. Still, Harish held on to his $6-per-hour job as a security guard in Somerset and made the hour-and-a-half nightly drives to and from work, while looking for another job during the day. He never found one.

Meanwhile, Zankhana and Kajal hated their schools, complaining of boredom and a lack of friends. In November 1991, the family returned to Edison, this time to a second-floor apartment in Hilltop Estates' building 25. Sharing a one-bedroom apartment once again, they took turns sleeping on a full-size bed in the bedroom, mattresses on the floor and the couch.

"Maybe we should go back to India," Harish said almost every day.

His daughters either ignored him or gave him a simple "No." Now it was too late. Zankhana was college bound and had more friends than she had ever had in her life. Kajal was just starting to make friends with the children in the neighborhood. Kapila just wanted the children to be happy.

They were getting used to life in America.

After graduation from Stevens in June 1992, Zankhana enrolled at Middlesex County College. Her father had hoped she would try to gain admission to Rutgers University at its flagship campus in New Brunswick or at least its Newark branch. But Zankhana's ranking in the bottom half of one of New Jersey's better high schools, coupled with the family's inability to afford tuition at a private college, forced her to attend community college. She studied business management and information technology and continued working as a cashier or clerk at fast-food eateries and stores.

In 1992, Harish was laid off from the security guard job. It had lasted more than two years, the longest he'd ever held a job in America. When Harish filed for unemployment, the unemployment officer told him that jobs were scarce and that all he could offer Harish was the chance to attend school. Harish jumped at the chance to learn basic computer skills at Middlesex County College. Here, he thought, was his chance to learn the things that would make him more marketable to an American bank. After a series of courses in Microsoft Office applications, Harish was hired in the consumer loan department of a First Fidelity Bancorp branch. He worked there until 1994, when the bank merged with First Union, resulting in thousands of layoffs in New Jersey. Harish enlisted with a temporary agency and spent the next year unsuccessfully looking for full-time work. The family depleted their savings and started to sink into credit card debt.

One day in early 1994, Zankhana went to bake after school at a friend's house, a girl who also lived in Hilltop. There, she met Harcharnjit Singh, a clean-shaven Sikh who had emigrated from Punjab in 1990, the same year she had. He was living with his sister in Carteret, a northeastern Middlesex County town on Staten Island Sound, but had lived with a group of Punjabis in Hilltop when he first came to America. With her friend entertaining her own boyfriend, Zankhana was left with Harcharnjit, known as Bittu. He spoke little English, so the two conversed in Hindi. At first they discussed this and that, but almost immediately Zankhana started to open up to him about how she felt caged at home and wanted out. That night, Bittu called Zankhana and asked her if she'd like to "hang out" again.

"I'll think about it," she said, her flirtatious laughter telling him she didn't have to. She didn't understand why she felt such an immediate attraction to Bittu. He was average looking and was rather chubby—Zankhana knew she could do better—and he certainly wasn't wealthy. But whenever Zankhana saw him, she ended up divulging all her problems, from the family's economic situation to stress over classes. "It's like our hearts just talk to each other," she once told him.

Zankhana never told her parents about Bittu, knowing they would disapprove of her relationship with a Sikh, albeit one who wasn't religious. Besides, Harish had always told Kajal and Zankhana they were not to date until they had finished college. Harish and Kapila never spelled out all the rules, but it was assumed the men their daughters married would have to meet with their approval in caste, profession, and character. Zankhana had no idea how Bittu—a New York City cabdriver who had only finished the seventh grade in India—would fare, but she feared not well. For Zankhana, who took classes and often worked more than one job, it was easy to sneak around without her parents knowing whom she was seeing. But with both Bittu and Zankhana having ties to Hilltop, their business soon became everyone's.

Six months after they began dating, Bittu asked Zankhana to marry him, and she accepted. Now she would have to tell her parents. Zankhana broke the news first to her mother, who immediately burst into tears. "I don't mind, but your father—he is not going to like this at all," Kapila said.

Zankhana waited to tell her father until a day when her uncles were visiting. She thought that if more people were around, he couldn't cause a scene.

"I have met the man I am going to marry," Zankhana announced.

She was greeted with silence, not the outrage she expected. Her uncle asked her to bring Bittu to meet the family the next day.

Upon meeting the twenty-four-year-old suitor, Harish and Kapila told their daughter and her boyfriend that they realized there was nothing they could do to stop them from marrying. Harish had just one request: "Please, I came here for my daughters' education and better life. All I ask is that you get married in one year, when she finishes her college." Inwardly, though, Harish couldn't help but think his daughter was too good for a cabdriver, and a Sikh one at that. Bittu and Zankhana agreed to Harish's condition.

That summer, the Patels took a family vacation to India, their first visit since they had left Baroda five years earlier. Kapila wanted to see her doctor—she had been to three different doctors in the United States who could not determine where her pain was coming from—and both daughters wanted to be with her. Harish had plans, too. Without telling Zankhana, he had arranged for her to meet potential husbands. Now he told her he wanted her to get married before they returned to the United States. "Zankhana, these guys here are better educated than Bittu," Harish pleaded. "I don't care about his caste or religion anymore, but he will not be able to do anything other than drive a taxi with his education."

Zankhana spent the rest of her vacation in India screaming, crying, and fighting with her parents. Seeing he could not force her, Harish agreed to allow her to return to the States as long as she kept to the original promise of waiting till her schooling was finished. The family returned to Edison in time for Kajal to begin her freshman year at Stevens. The fights persisted, however, and a few months later Zankhana left home, dropped out of school just one semester shy of graduation, quit her job at Stern's department store, and moved into Bittu's sister's apartment in Carteret.

Her parents begged her to return, but Zankhana felt she couldn't trust them anymore after what Harish had said in India. Meanwhile, Bittu's parents were rejecting the idea of their son marrying Zankhana, a Hindu. Bittu and Zankhana said they felt neither family would accept the other. "All we can do is do it ourselves," Zankhana told him.

On Christmas Eve 1995, they were wed at a Sikh gurdwara, or temple, in Bridgewater. No family members from the Patels' side were present for the ceremony. Bittu's brother-in-law said Harish would probably cause a scene and ruin the day for everyone.

Zankhana did not wear the traditionally ornate sari or twenty-two-carat gold jewelry typical of Hindu weddings. She tried to hold her tears inside as a handful of her husband's family wished the couple well. Unlike her parents' wedding twenty-five years earlier, which consisted of several religious rites over a three-day period, Zankhana's entire wedding lasted about three hours.

On their wedding night, Bittu and Zankhana climbed the stairs to the one-bedroom apartment they had rented near his sister's. Bittu opened the door to their new home, bare of furnishings—not even two pillows like those Zankhana's parents had given their daughters to sleep upon more than five years earlier. They spread out bedsheets on the living room floor. And as she had five years ago, Zankhana took her place on the floor and went to sleep, unsure of what was to come.

3

A Gold-Paved Entry

The royal treatment started with Sankumani Sarma's first visit to the United States. It was August 1995, and he and five others were on a business trip to Grand Rapids, Michigan, visiting the headquarters of Steelcase, Inc., a furniture manufacturer, to observe its process of making office chairs. Steelcase gave each a daily coupon to dine in the cafeteria. There was no amount listed, no limitations on their intake. Instead, the visitors' tickets were stamped with the words "'Til you're satisfied."

Sanku and his friends took the words to heart. They made repeated trips to the counter, filled up cups of coffee, sampled juices from apple to orange, tried mashed potatoes for the first time. Calculatingly, they tried to eat three meals in that one sitting. Their own employer, a major Indian furniture manufacturer, had given each a $45 daily allowance for meals and expenses. Rather than spend the money—at the time, $45 was more than a thousand rupees, more than a week's salary—Sanku and his roommate stocked up on loaves of bread and bananas and ate them for dinner in their room at the Holiday Inn. To get to their destinations, the Indians walked across highways, hurdling concrete medians along the way, rather than taking a cab. They scrimped on expenses wherever possible, hoping to stretch the dollars and spend them on gifts for their wives or girlfriends, mothers and cousins. After all, one could not visit America and not bring back the brand names to prove it.

Sanku ventured out once on his own, taking the hotel shuttle to the nearest mall. He entered the mall through Best Buy, the singer in him lingering in its music and stereo section. Then he made his way through the mall, buying Lipi a few silk nighties, a dish set, and a pair of earrings. And he exited the mall.

Everything looked the same yet somehow different, Sanku thought. White lines for parking spots, purposefully planted trees, endless rows of cars. But where was Best Buy? Where was the shuttle? He walked around for twenty minutes with no luck. Finally a police officer stopped and asked if Sanku was lost and needed help.

Sanku hopped into the squad car and arrived at the entrance to Best Buy and the stop in a matter of seconds. But the last shuttle had just left.

Panicked, Sanku flagged down a man driving a van and asked for a ride to the Holiday Inn. The man appeared scared and hesitant but, after looking at Sanku's own terrified expression, told him to hop in. They drove in an awkward silence, no talk of the weather, their homes or plans.

Back at the hotel, Sanku was able to laugh at his day in America, like one he'd never lived before. *The driver seemed so scared of me. He didn't even say a word. But that policeman was actually helpful. That never would have happened in India.*

It was a thought that resounded more than once during Sanku's first trip to America. At the Steelcase plant, he noticed the very specific compartmentalization of jobs. *One guy does de-*

sign, another does parts, a few perform assembly, a separate company handles marketing and advertising. Why, in India, I'd make the whole chair and then take it to market. Here, I could spend my days making castors and be home by five o'clock. The designs in America also seemed more original, unlike the copycat models passed off in India.

There were other differences. Once, the Indian group was scheduled to meet with Steelcase executives at 2:00 P.M. Much to Sanku's amazement, the meeting really started at 2:00! In India, Sanku's meetings always were on IST, Indian Standard Time, loosely defined to be anywhere from twenty minutes to two hours after whatever time the boss called a meeting for.

Of course, slowly, changes were entering India's marketplace. In fact, Sanku's very trip was made possible by the economic reforms sweeping India. His employer in Bombay, Godrej & Boyce, had recently entered into a partnership with Steelcase that allowed its products to be manufactured and sold by Godrej. Despite a century spent as the market leader, Steelcase had not been able to penetrate India because of high duties on imported goods.

That changed in 1991, when after decades of protectionism India opened its borders to the world and paved the way for foreign investment and imports from cars to computers to enter the world's second most populous country. The economic "liberalization" slowly created an India familiar to many Americans, complete with milkshakes, MTV, and M&M's. The result was also a consumer culture obsessed with the West, one that valued day-to-day time-savers and conveniences such as Kellogg's cereal for breakfast instead of egg curries and fresh roti.

Indeed, Sanku and Lipi considered themselves members of that emerging middle class, estimated at more than 200 million people. In Bombay, they grew accustomed to the use of credit cards and dined at five-star hotels. (Indians still call restaurants "hotels" because hotels used to be among the few places besides home to enjoy a sit-down meal.) More than half of Bombay's dwellers, by some estimates, live in slums. In the words of Indian writer Suketu Mehta, the movie, fashion, and financial capital is "India's collective dream of itself." For centuries, the poor and well-to-do, the skilled and unskilled, arrived in the port city in search of riches and opportunity, hoping the old saying would ring true: "No one in Bombay sleeps on an empty stomach."

Sanku and Lipi much preferred the fast-paced life of Bombay to their native region, the sleepier province of Assam. Known best for its production of tea and for the vast, winding Brahmaputra River, Assam was home to a decades-old separatist movement. To conduct business or work there, one had to cope with frequent bandhs, or strikes, that forced the closure of all normal activity and business. The reforms changing the rest of India were slow to gain ground in Assam, further fueling the militants' claims, and neither Sanku nor Lipi saw a future there for themselves. Born after India's independence, they had few qualms about liberalization and felt it had impacted their lives quite positively.

It took nearly fifty years for India to shed a wary attitude toward the West. After all, to convince the nation it did not have to remain a British colony, Gandhi had preached self-sufficiency, wearing the homespun khadi as he led the infamous salt marches to sea. His philosophy led to independence, but some argue it laid the groundwork for an overprotective government. To be sure, the Indian government embarked on liberalization unwillingly. In 1991, the nation found itself in financial crisis, its foreign exchange reserves nearly depleted. To qualify for World Bank and International Monetary Fund loans, India agreed to open its economy. That summer, the newly installed government of Prime Minister Narasimha Rao devalued the rupee and lowered taxes and tariffs on imports.

The results were dramatic. Between 1994 and 1997, India's economy grew at an unprecedented 7 percent annually—this after decades of 3.5 percent increases, a so-called Hindu rate of growth. While deregulation made rapid changes, they didn't come fast enough for some citizens and companies. The Indian government placed tough local ownership restrictions on multinational companies from McDonald's to Revlon to Steelcase. That was what led the U.S.-based furniture giant to Sanku's company.

In India, Godrej is a household name, enjoying a brand-name success akin to that of Kleenex or Xerox in the United States: while the company makes all types of furniture, "a Godrej" has come to signify the large metal armoire Indians keep in their bedrooms. With its keys tucked into the creases of a matriarch's sari, the Godrej holds a bride's trousseau, her gold, her newest saris, the household cash. A bride's parents usually give a newly married couple their Godrej, along with the rest of the bedroom set.

As a company, Godrej exemplifies the conglomerates that were seen as the lifetime employers of choice, perhaps a close second to a civil service job with the government. Family-run companies such as Tata and Birla make everything from shoes to trucks. Godrej's products also run the gamut from soap to rocket engines, but it remains best known for the large armoire, along with other household items and office equipment, such as refrigerators and typewriters.

Thanks to his job as a designer at Godrej, Sanku and Lipi lived in the company's housing complex just yards away from its gated headquarters in the Pirojshahnagar neighborhood of Vikholi, a section of Bombay. Bombay's real estate crunch is often compared to Manhattan's, and often concluded to be worse, so large employers like Godrej provide subsidized housing for employees complete with cricket fields, playgrounds, and other recreational areas. The Godrej complex where Sanku and Lipi lived was known as Hill Side Colony, and their apartment building indeed sat on a rolling hill among other mounds of homes scattered in lush trees and vegetation. Sanku rode his Suzuki motorbike to work, while Lipi, a software consultant, squeezed her way onto a crowded train or bus to get to her office. On lucky days, she rode home in the company's air-conditioned Jeep.

Sanku's visit to Michigan that summer of 1995 did wonders for his confidence. Despite the razzle-dazzle life in Bombay he and Lipi had grown accustomed to, he had been intimidated by the idea of going to the United States. America had remained a mystery, a place he'd seen in movies and on television. He had a sister who lived in California, but she and her husband said little about the life they lived abroad. In fact, he had had a chance to immigrate in 1990, when he was admitted to a graduate program in design at Arizona State University, but he had no way of affording a hefty tuition bill that would surely have been in the tens of thousands of dollars. After his visit, Sanku realized he too could make America his home.

Upon his return to Bombay, Sanku told Lipi about his experiences. She laughed at the image of him lost in the mall and riding around in a police car.

"I think we'd be happy there," Sanku said.

Lipi too had been noticing that a lot of her classmates from Assam Engineering College in Guwahati, Assam's largest city, were emigrating from India on the H-1B visa. After six months as an instrumentation engineer at the Schlumberger Corporation, she had just spent another year taking courses at the National Center for Software Technology. She was about to start a programming job at Tata Consultancy Services, a subsidiary of India's biggest conglomerate, and knew that would make her among those most coveted by U.S. employers.

"I can easily go to America with my job," she told him. "But maybe you want to look into what you can do."

Sanku knew she was right. Godrej wasn't about to open a U.S. plant anytime soon. The visas everyone kept talking about applied mostly to software engineers or computer programmers; he was an office equipment designer. His sister in California told him sponsoring family members for immigration wasn't as easy as it used to be in the 1980s.

To get to America, he would just have to change careers, Sanku thought matter-of-factly. Perhaps he reasoned this way because he had always had an easy time switching modes; he studied civil engineering as an undergraduate and then transferred to industrial design for his master's degree at the prestigious Indian Institute of Technology in Bombay.

In India, IIT is as familiar a name as Harvard in the United States. With the wave of software engineers graduated from the IITs entering the United States, it also gained a reputation among American companies. Prominent IIT grads in the United States today include Vinod Khosla, cofounder of Sun Microsystems; Rajat Gupta, managing director of McKinsey & Co.; and Victor Menezes, chairman and CEO of Citibank.

In some ways, gaining admission to one of the six IITs resembled qualifying for the Olympics. The Bombay IIT's industrial design program only had fifteen spots each year, and thousands of people applied for them. In the twenty-five-year history of the program, Sanku had heard that only one civil engineering major had been admitted—ironically, another Assamese. Sanku knew why; civil engineering often had little to do with the actual design of a product. It was easy to see how architects and materials engineers might be preferred. Still, he applied, knowing admission to this program might be his only ticket out of a field he had studied for four years but really didn't like. He had a job pending in New Delhi, but it only offered 1,500 rupees monthly. Ironically, Sanku had majored in civil engineering as an undergraduate because his father had told him it was the only thing he could use to get back to Assam, a region slow to embrace the tech boom. Now, Sanku wanted to do everything in his power to ensure he didn't have to return home.

In 1988, as Sanku applied for the IIT program, he took a test known as the CEED, or combined entrance examination for design. The exam was easy, asking him to do simple tasks such as to create graphic images out of eight sticks. The difficult part was the in-person interviews in Bombay. By the time Sanku learned he had been invited, he was surprised he'd made it so far and figured he still had no chance of being among the lucky fifteen. By that time, Sanku assumed all he'd get out of the whole experience was a free trip to Bombay.

He arrived on the Friday before his Monday interview. His first stop was the campus bookstore, where he asked for any books related to the industrial design sequence at the university. Given a third semester text on "ergonomics," a term he had never encountered before, Sanku quickly leafed through it. Convinced he would not be admitted, Sanku spent the weekend "boozing out" and touring Bombay for only the second time in his life.

During his interview, a half-dozen academics fired questions at him, mostly focusing on why an engineering major would suddenly want to enter a graduate course in design. Inwardly, Sanku thought, *Anything is better than civil engineering*. To the panel, he professed his interest in the field of ergonomics and threw in a few other technical terms he'd learned in his review of the textbook the night before.

When the list of admitted candidates went up later that week, Sankumani Sarma was among the fifteen.

After graduating from IIT, Sanku took the job at Godrej and quickly moved up its ranks. He married Lipi in 1994, an arranged marriage arranged in an unusual way.

Sanku's father had gone to the home of one of Lipi's engineering-college classmates to inquire about this girl as a possible match for his son. She informed him she had just gotten engaged.

"But wait," she said. "I have this friend, Shravani Phukan." She assured Sanku's father her friend was also a Brahmin and also very nice. She passed along Lipi's phone number and parents' names. When Sanku's father left, she immediately ran to the phone.

Lipi's adamant response: "I am *not* marrying anybody named Sankumani." "Mani" attached to a name is a sign of affection in Assamese, akin to calling a grown man "Mikey."

But when he came with his father to meet her, Lipi and her relatives were immediately impressed. As a modernizing India still practices the centuries-old practice of arranged marriage, men increasingly bring their friends along to check out a prospective bride. That Sanku—who lived in Bombay!—came with his father showed his traditional Assamese values. As soon as the families sat down—the Sarmas on one side, the Phukans on the other—Sanku's father gestured to Lipi.

"I see a room over there. Why don't you take him in there and talk for a while?"

In the room, Sanku and Lipi chatted. He asked her the requisite "Can you cook?" and she responded with her planned answer of "Of course not." He asked her about her courses; she asked him about living in Bombay. He told her he liked to sing, that he'd even performed on All-India Radio and had been a headliner at college functions. Ten minutes later, they emerged. When the Sarmas left, Lipi told her parents she would marry Sanku. On the ride back to their house in Guwahati, Sanku told his father the same.

Their courtship lasted four months, mostly long distance. Sanku returned to Bombay and wrote Lipi long letters alternating lines about his latest weekend excursion with words professing his love for her. She responded occasionally and tersely. They spoke by phone sometimes, and in those conversations, too, Lipi remained matter-of-fact, while Sanku was the romantic.

After their wedding in Jorhat, a city in Upper Assam, they had a one-night honeymoon in Shillong, a resort in the nearby hills. Sanku would have liked to take her to the much grander Kashmir or Simla or Goa, but he had no money left, having chosen to spend it on a brand-new television and a secondhand stereo. After their night in Shillong, they left for their new home in Bombay.

Lipi went to work at Schlumberger and then, in early 1996, joined Tata Consultancy Services, which was the local company working with Nortel Networks. Companies entering India helped transform the workplace in many ways; air-conditioning and wall-to-wall carpeting became commonplace, for example. But the nature of high-tech firms and their young work forces also had a liberalizing effect—similar to the laid-back atmosphere of dot-coms in the United States. Tata, more than a century old, underwent dramatic changes during India's tech boom. Gone were the days of calling bosses "sir" and office assistants "peons." When she brought her father, visiting from Assam, to work, he was amazed at how Lipi addressed her group leader, a young man named Suhas. "How can you call him Suhas, not sir?" Even the executive office was affected; sometime after Lipi left, the CEO of Tata Consultancy changed his memo headings from "Office Orders" to "From the CEO's desk."

Clients from overseas increasingly came to meet with Lipi's bosses to discuss outsourcing big projects. Often, she laughed to herself at their outdated notions of India as the land of snake charmers, the Taj Mahal, and oppressed women. Perhaps it was because she and most other women in the office still wore salwar kameezes to work; the only ones who wore pants were the Parsis; Parsi women in Bombay are known for being headstrong and well educated. Once a male client from Canada asked if it was okay to shake her hand. She obliged, giving him a firm grip, then turned the conversation to his company's information technology needs. Clients would spell out demands for a product, then Indian programmers would write the code. So-called back office functions were much cheaper when performed by a programmer such as Lipi, who earned 23,000 rupees per month, at the time about $575, at Tata. Her U.S. counterpart likely earned more than $50,000 per year. While India graduated two and a half times as many software engineers as the United States annually, one study found the Indians were paid one-fifth to one-tenth of their American counterparts' salaries. These software engineers know they are seen as cheap labor by the United States, but in India their salaries get them large flats, fast cars, and a comfortable lifestyle complete with maids, cooks, and drivers.

In the United States, meanwhile, some Indian programmers also accused employers of paying them less than Americans. Despite H-1B holders' gripes, the U.S. Labor Department documented few complaints. It reportedly received sixty-three complaints in 1998, compared to forty-eight the previous year. However, a study commissioned by the Labor Department in 1996 found that 19 percent of H-1B workers were not receiving the wages to which they were entitled. The study said the government's role amounted to little more than stamping applications for visas and looking the other way once workers arrived. "The system is complaint-driven, and not too many of these affected workers want to complain," John Fraser, deputy wage and hour administrator at the Labor Department, told *Computerworld*.

In the global crunch for information technology workers, India was ready to supply. Much of India's population was educated in English-speaking schools set up by the British government or Christian missionaries. The economic liberalization that started in 1991 allowed for the mass import of computers and equipment. Young Indians began to see a future in their country's burgeoning software industry, naming the southern city of Bangalore its own "Silicon Plateau" and a section of Hyderabad "Cyberabad." Sanku's alma mater, IIT, was emblematic of a rigid university system that churned out thousands of qualified technical people every year. Meanwhile, India's geographic position offered a time-zone advantage over Europe and North America, enabling software engineers to remotely maintain information technology and operating systems while their clients slept. Often, American clients would leave their offices after e-mailing instructions to India before their dinner hour, then return the next morning to find the task completed.

Besides an increased workload and competing job offers on Indian soil, Lipi started to see more and more of her colleagues enticed by the prospect of America. Even the most talented of her college classmates, known as the "toppers," who she never thought would leave, were saying good-bye to India for better opportunities abroad; this phenomenon became known as the "brain drain." They learned the alphabet soup–lined path that leads to the United States: GRE, TOEFL, and H-1B. Most cited their desire to leave India as a testament to the country's ultimate failure to offer its software engineers more lucrative salaries and opportunities. To young professionals, India's expanding software sector became their ticket out.

But Sanku and Lipi weren't quite ready to leave. They were members of Bombay's rising "dink" class: double income, no kids. They saw a future in the software companies entering India, as well as those homegrown ventures cropping up to meet demand. They spent weekends taking day trips to the beaches along the coast, Sanku driving the Suzuki with Lipi holding on as her hair, as short as his, flapped in the wind. They often spent nights on the beach.

Even though theirs had been an arranged marriage, their love had grown intensely. Sanku sang songs in Hindi and Assamese to Lipi as they sat on the beach and inhaled the salty air of the Indian Ocean. Sometimes, she joined him for a duet.

In late 1996, Sanku saw an advertisement for a three-week computer course offered by Microsoft. This was his chance. He told his boss that he was going home to Assam for three weeks. Instead, Sanku left each morning on his motorbike for the day-long Microsoft classes. Because he and Lipi lived in an apartment complex where so many of his co-workers also resided, he sneaked out each morning, donning his helmet even before walking out the door.

On June 28, 1997, Lipi gave birth to a baby boy, Chiku. Still, they weren't ready to leave. Lipi didn't want to go until Chiku was a year old.

By 1997, Indians and Chinese together comprised nearly half of the 65,000 immigrants who entered the American workforce on an H-1B visa. The next largest group of workers—just under 8,000—was from Japan. H-1B recipients were a special breed of immigrant, coveted by high-tech firms in America who claimed recruiting workers from abroad helped combat a labor shortage in the software industry. The visa program allowed the imported workers to stay in the United States for six years. It became an easy way for natives of countries such as India, Russia, China, and the United Kingdom to land in the United States, bypassing lengthy application processes for more permanent working visas. In fact, through the late 1990s, most professional high-tech, finance, or health-care workers from abroad came to the United States under the H-1B program. The visa was issued to those with at least a bachelor's degree and "highly technical" or "specialized" skills, in the language of the INS.

In 1998, Lipi started fielding offers from software consulting firms willing to sponsor her immigration to the United States. She marveled at how the companies seemed almost hungry for bodies who knew C or C++ code, computer programs used for an array of network functions. It came at just the right time. The hustle and bustle of Bombay was beginning to wear on both her and Sanku, and they remembered the saying among Indians, "If you can make it in Bombay, you can make it anywhere." Lipi's commute was getting longer and longer; suddenly, traveling thirty miles in two hours was considered good time, and the pollution hung thick over the ocean and skyline they once loved. Their trips home to Assam were sixty hours by train; plane tickets were too expensive. "We're already so far from our parents," Lipi said to Sanku. "Why not just go to America?"

Until the end of 1998, the United States had a cap of 65,000 on the number of H-1B visas issued per year, a quota that had gone unfulfilled. Then the Internet and information technology revolutions exploded, and H-1B visas were exhausted in a little more than seven months. American companies, specifically the surge of start-ups, suddenly found themselves scrambling to fill a labor shortage. In 1999, Congress—succumbing to the heat of the computer lobby—upped the quota to 115,000 but also, concerned about taking jobs away from Americans, legislated that the cap would drop to 107,500 in 2001 and back to 65,000 in 2002.

High-tech recruiters continued to lobby. Their opponents remained equally vociferous, saying efforts should be made to cultivate a homegrown techie workforce. In 1998, as the Sarmas started to field their first offers via e-mail accounts in Bombay, Representative Sheila Jackson Lee, a black Democrat from Texas, testified before a House Immigration Committee hearing on the matter. She advocated recruiting from historically black colleges. "Not one Silicon Valley firm recruited during the 1998 conference of the National Council of Black Scientists and Engineers in Oakland, California," she said. "Only two Silicon Valley firms fund scholarships through the National Action Council for Minorities in Engineering, which provides assistance to 10 percent of all underrepresented group students in engineering. And the National Society of Black Engineers of Silicon Valley has only four corporate sponsors."

In early 1999, Lipi accepted a job with Global Consultants in Parsippany, a so-called body shop that would then lease Lipi, with her skills and knowledge of various computer languages, out to another company. Sanku had received no offers in the meantime, so he accepted the first one he did get: a job teaching Microsoft applications at a computer institute in Edison.

On a February morning, Lipi lined up at the U.S. Consulate in the ritzy Breach Candy section of Bombay. Although she had heard rumors of queues that snaked around the block with people camped out at 3:00 A.M., Lipi, holding Chiku in her arms, arrived at 8:00 A.M. for the 8:30 opening and was surprised to see it not so crowded. She received a coupon and waited for their number to be called. For H-1B approval, a candidate must submit a letter issued by the Immigration and Naturalization Service and proof of U.S. employment. Sanku had gone the week before and gotten his visa approved without a problem. They didn't even ask him any questions. Lipi was a different story.

The officer asked to see her salary slips from her old job. Luckily, Lipi had brought every form of paperwork she had imagined they would want. They asked whom she would be traveling with, and she gestured at Chiku. She showed them his passport. She felt nervous.

"What about your husband?"

"He got his H-1 last week." Lipi was worried that they weren't going to be allowed to immigrate all together. She and Sanku had seen some couples send one spouse first, and others go ahead and leave their child with a grandparent or aunt. Early on, though, the Sarmas resolved to go together or not at all.

The officer stood up and yelled for his supervisor. "Mom and Dad are both going on H-1. What do I do for the kiddo?"

Lipi panicked. *What if they wouldn't let Chiku go?*

"Give him an H-4" was the response, meaning a dependent's visa.

Once they asked for payment of fees—about $45 for the visa and $100 for processing—Lipi breathed easier.

After their visas had been processed, their departure took place over a matter of days. Lipi's parents came out from Assam to bid them farewell. Originally, she was going to ask them to accompany her and Sanku, fearing she couldn't trust anyone in America to watch her son.

"If you need us to go, we'll go," said Lipi's mother. "But we might be more of a problem, a burden on you there." Lipi decided she was right.

As they said good-bye, Lipi's mother wondered how big her grandson would be the next time she saw him. She imagined the stages of his growth she would miss, his first words, his first steps. She wondered if her daughter would ever return.

At Bombay's airport, only Lipi's brother came to see them off. Lipi didn't cry, nor did Sanku. "We were scared, of course," Lipi said later. "There's a fear of the unknown. But there's also a knowledge that if it doesn't work, we can come back."

March 3, 1999, was a cold, rainy day. The British Airways flight carrying the Sarma family landed at Newark International Airport about 5:00 P.M. under a sky that looked gray and imposing.

Upon exiting customs, Lipi panicked. Her waist pouch, containing $150 and about 5,000 rupees—she had it on the plane—*where was it now?* She checked her handbag and purse. Sanku didn't have it. Lipi realized she had left it in the seat pocket in front of her.

Sanku was not understanding. "How could you do that?" he scolded. "We're not even here one hour and you're already losing money."

"Don't yell at me," Lipi snapped back. "I'm feeling bad enough about it."

She stopped a woman wearing a British Airways uniform and asked how she could track down her pouch. "Just wait here. I'm going to go radio the pilot," the woman said.

The ten minutes the Sarmas waited seemed eternal to Lipi. They didn't have much cash on them, and at this hour, where could they cash their travelers' checks? *This must be a bad omen. Perhaps they weren't supposed to have come. It had all been so quick.*

Then the woman returned with the pouch. She asked Lipi to describe it and handed it back to her. Lipi counted the money within—intact. She felt better about America.

As they left the airport, the sun was beginning to set, and the instant cold shocked them. Lipi tried to let her mind go blank, almost as if to allow her surroundings and impressions to seep into her. A black Lincoln Town Car awaited, its driver carrying a placard with "SHRAVANI SARMA" in bold capital letters, He drove them to a motel, the Budget Inn in Parsippany, where they were to live for two weeks. For H-1B's, this period was known as being "on the bench," techie parlance for awaiting placement in a company.

Once at the motel, Lipi felt insecure. They had no car, no way out of their room. Their Thomas Cook travelers' checks were not widely accepted. Lipi called up the Prasads, a South Indian couple in Edison whose number she'd been given by friends in Bombay, and asked for help.

As soon as the Prasads came and picked Lipi and Sanku up, they began an orientation to life in the United States. That first weekend, Lipi and Sanku stayed with the Prasads, heavily relying on the South Indian couple for advice on what clothes to buy, what town to live in, what banks and credit card companies to sign up with. Their first stops were Kmart and Wal-Mart. The first purchase Lipi made was a rice cooker. For Chiku, she bought jackets and pullovers made of fleece, a material she'd never seen before.

A friend back in India had given Lipi the name of an Assamese couple who lived in the same apartment complex as the Prasads, Durham Woods, notable as the site of a pipeline explosion and devastating fire in 1994. She dialed the number for Ram and Sunita Dhar, who invited them out that very night for a get-together at another friend's house.

That night, Sanku and Lipi met more Assamese than they had in years. The conversation turned to a cultural function that was coming up. Some of the group wanted to put together a chorus to perform at it, but they had no harmonium player and no lead singer. Eagerly, Sanku told them of his abilities.

On his fifteenth day in America, Sanku felt stir-crazy in the motel. He took a bus—buses seemed to run only sporadically in the suburbs, he noticed—to a row of car dealers and bought a secondhand Ford Tempo for less than $6,000, using the motel as his primary address and showing them his international driver's license. Without a job, credit history, or address, even a New Jersey driver's license, Sanku bought a car.

I'm really in America now.

The next step was to find a place to live. With the three of them in the motel room, any annoyance, not to mention the baby's crying, was heightened. Again, they turned to the Prasads.

The Edison the Sarmas encountered in 1999 epitomized just how immigrants had changed suburbia. The 1990 census showed that nearly 20,000 Asian Indians were among the 671,000 residents in Middlesex County. Yet the suburbs posed unique challenges to new immigrants, especially the cash-strapped. Public transportation was scarce, so they either walked or stuffed themselves into makeshift taxis and vans. Ethnic enclaves initially were more spread out, and while the more entrenched helped the newer arrivals—as the Prasads did the Sarmas—there were clear divisions based on class, region, and educational level. Eventually, the older developments, such as Hilltop Estates and sections of Durham Woods, became known as areas for the recent arrivals or those who couldn't get out. Meanwhile, New Jersey's green spaces continued to be developed at an alarming pace. New housing divisions, from condominiums to townhouses to "McMansions," sprawled across Edison and Woodbridge, East Brunswick and Bridgewater.

On March 26, the Sarmas moved into their first home in America, a spacious one-bedroom apartment in Village Common, a new housing development in Edison with pink bricks and eggshell-colored aluminum siding. On a sunny day, Village Common resembled a retirement community in Florida. Lipi and Sanku were pleased that their new home was bigger than the one they'd had in Bombay, but they missed the sense of community created by parks and cricket fields and colleagues who worked and lived together. Even their son felt life had changed quite significantly. When Chiku entered and saw the empty apartment, he cried, "Where's my bed? My TV?"

Soon afterward, Lipi came off the bench into a job at AT&T. She marveled at the number of Indians like her on staff. There were many Chinese as well, but they mostly spoke in Mandarin together; the Indians preferred English. At lunch, the ethnic groups dined separately in the company cafeteria. Lipi thought it was weird. *Why, there was more intermingling in India!* One study of immigrants from China and India in Silicon Valley found the two groups organized quite separately and distinctly from one another, with little overlap. There, meetings of the Monte Jade Science and Technology Association and North American Taiwanese Engineers Association spoke Mandarin Chinese at meetings, for example, excluding even the Chinese who spoke Cantonese or those from Hong Kong.

Sanku also started his job at Microsoft, teaching from 8:00 A.M. to 1:00 P.M. and then 6:00 P.M. to 10:00 P.M. With one car, the couple was always at the mercy of their South Indian friends for a ride to work or to pick up Chiku at daycare.

In April 1999, they attended Bohag Bihu, a spring holiday celebrated widely throughout Assam to commemorate a harvest. Lipi sought out Pronoti Dutta, a woman who grew up with Lipi's mother in Jorhat. Upon hearing of their connection, Pronoti enveloped Lipi in her famous bear hug and vowed to take care of her. Sanku's voice made him was an instant hit in the tight-knit Assamese community in New Jersey. Soon dinner invitations started pouring in, from new arrivals just like the Sarmas and from families settled in the United States for decades. Lipi and Sanku felt as if they had more Assamese friends here than in Bombay. In fact, Lipi found a car of her own, a Toyota, through a fellow Assamese who was moving to California—the end to the couple's commuting woes. She found a Punjabi nanny who would watch Chiku during the day, paying her about $200 a week. In the beginning, they multiplied every dollar by forty rupees and felt quite stingy. Three months after coming to America, they started dividing rupees by dollars.

Quickly, Lipi and Sanku settled into life in America, never ceasing to marvel at the speed of their adjustment. Lipi occasionally thought about how she never had to wash dishes or work as a cashier like some of the older immigrants they were friends with. But she felt she and Sanku made sacrifices of a different kind. Life in America with a kid was downright hard when both parents worked. In India, child care consisted of a nanny who earned 1,800 rupees per month, or about $45 at the time. In America, daycare was a huge portion of her paycheck. And when Lipi put Chiku down to bed at night, she never felt she had spent quite enough time with him. Chiku had come to America with few toys, but soon the apartment was strewn with Mickey Mouse and Barney paraphernalia, admittedly gifts purchased by his parents out of guilt. Lipi started to monitor Chiku's television viewing, allowing only Nickelodeon or the Cartoon Network. He wasn't allowed to watch the news. He wasn't allowed to play with guns. Lipi couldn't tell if she suddenly obsessed over her son's welfare because they were in America now or because he was growing up.

In July, Sanku was hired by AT&T, where Lipi was working, to do production support. "It's not a bad job," he told Lipi. "But it doesn't have a future. There's no opportunity to advance."

Lipi sighed. She felt similarly. Her work was pretty easy, but she always felt she was being fleeced. *If you make $70,000, they make $70,000 on top of that,* she often thought. *H-1B people don't really seem to have a career. They jump from job to job.* In their first few months, Lipi and Sanku began looking elsewhere for better-paying jobs. The H-1 program does not allow workers to be promoted if it means a change in their job description, and it is for this reason that H-1B workers tend to look for new jobs—and a transfer of the visa sponsorship—so often.

By the time they celebrated their one-year anniversary in America, Lipi had given Global Consultants, the body shop, the green light to file a green card application for her and Sanku. They had wanted to wait to see if they liked living in the States and until they made more money, but everyone told them the procedure took so long that they might as well get it started. The process began with labor certification, essentially proving that no native American could perform the jobs Lipi and Sanku could. Obtaining a green card for H-1B's also poses difficulty because, while the vast majority of the visas go to workers from India and China, the law states that only 7 percent of employment-based green cards can go to applicants from one source country annually. By the time they applied, the Sarmas knew they would be waiting years for their slot, years for the day they could switch jobs freely, for the day they knew they could stay in America.

Lipi and Sanku commuted together until August 2000, when Lipi transferred to Lucent, an AT&T spinoff that employed thousands throughout central New Jersey. Her manager at AT&T, an Indian man named Ashwin, was so sorry to see her go that he told her to call him if things didn't work out at Lucent.

The temporary visa program illustrated the dearth of high-tech labor in the United States, while seemingly keeping U.S. immigration doors open. Yet the very nature of the visa, temporary, underscored just how welcome people like Lipi and Sanku were—or were not. For them, getting fired or quitting would mean immediate deportation. No job, no visa. From the very beginning, Sanku and Lipi wondered whether they should purchase a home, because their temporary status made planning the long-term future quite difficult. In June 2000, one editorial writer summarized the predicament: "They are not full Americans, and they never can be."

Sanku and Lipi asked themselves and each other the question often. Could they ever be Americans? And if they could, did they even want to be?

4

Exercising Rights

As October 31 approaches, Harish takes the newspaper and skips straight to the classifieds—the real estate section, the employment section. He wants to leave Bradlees for a job that pays at least $12 an hour. He wants to leave this apartment with all its glaring imperfections from the trickle of water pressure he showers under to the flickering lights he switches off before bed.

There are more things he should change but cannot afford to. The old television, its wavy lines of reception caught off rabbit ears wrapped in tinfoil. The fraying carpet, not quite cut to any room's size, exposing hardwood no realtor would boast about. The plaid seat cushions on the couch, shredded to the point of exposing a yellow foam. Zankhana, on a trip home recently, took one look and drove Kapila straight to the mall. They purchased a checkered bedsheet and a plain purple one. "It's important to have contrast in a room," Zankhana said as she slipped the solid sheet onto a loveseat and the checkered one onto Harish's easy chair.

The cloth shrouds the ripped couches like a Band-Aid on a cut, a temporary cover for a wound everyone knows exists.

Harish pays $850 monthly for the one-bedroom apartment. To upgrade to a two-bedroom, as he's been meaning to for a decade now, is a difference of $300, a difference he can't afford. There's no air-conditioning. In the winter, the heat is sweltering; they open the balcony door to let cool air in.

Such is the condition of the apartments in Hilltop Estates. Admittedly, Hilltop's inhabitants are not wealthy. Not everyone has a car, usually a necessity in these parts. They hang their dhotis and saris out on clotheslines not only to avoid shrinkage but also to save quarters. They cram as many as ten people into an apartment—usually extended family—and take turns sleeping on mattresses strewn about the floor. Rare is the living room in Hilltop that doesn't have mattresses propped up against the walls. Belongings spill out onto balconies: bookcases, end tables, folding chairs for company; the Patels store Kajal's old bike, bags of rice, old sneakers, and a vacuum cleaner on theirs. Thrift, however, has its exceptions. Many of these apartments have satellite dishes affixed atop their roofs or protruding sideways from windows and balconies. Teenage daughters shell out nearly $10 each weekend to see hunky heart-throb Aamir Khan's new movie or former Miss World Aishwarya Rai's exposed navel swaying to the latest beat. They spend $15 to get their eyebrows and upper lips threaded—a hair removal method favored by Indians—for special occasions; if they're lucky, their neighbor knows how and will do it for free. Most of the residents are Gujaratis, identifiable by the way they drape their sari's paloo over their right side and the languages they speak in the laundry room to one another, and on the playground to their children. Many are Gujaratis from the Kheda district, who came in on tourist visas to visit family and overstayed their official welcome.

Gujarat is one of the top sources for immigration to the United States; Gujuratis comprise just 5 percent of India's population but an estimated 20 percent of the Indian population in the United States. Their large numbers enable the creation of mini-Gujarati communities in the subdivisions of central New Jersey, most notably Hilltop Estates. In the same greetings and farewells employed in the villages and cities of Gujarat, conversations begin with a salutation of "Kem cho" and end with "Jai Shri Krishna" or "Jai Shri Swaminarayan." The latter phrases loosely translate into "May [whichever deity is worshiped] be with you."

Visitors to Hilltop notice right away its large concentration of elderly residents, the women known as behenjis, who travel in packs. They take walks in the evenings, more so in the summer months. On the crisp fall days of late, they cram socked or stockinged feet into leather chappals with a space for one big bare toe. Their purpose in immigrating to America so late in life is entirely utilitarian. Grandmothers and grandfathers can babysit during the day and help a working mother get dinner on the table at night. Often they come because there's no life left for them in India. In a traditional Indian household, the eldest son takes over control of the parents' estate, dividing property among the remaining brothers. Because Gujarati immigrants tend to sponsor siblings once in the United States, many homes have been left without an heir apparent in India, so the only solution is to bring over parents, too.

The older immigrants often find themselves giving up freedom and their role at the head of the family, as they are at the mercy of sons and daughters who can drive, speak English, and navigate America. Senior centers nationwide have had to adapt to their own newcomers, mixing bridge and bingo with Afghan exercise hour in Fremont, California, or adding Buddhist meditation and vegetarian meals in the case of the Edison center. Loneliness and depression often mark the experiences of senior immigrants, who find themselves homebound in a foreign land. In some ways, Hilltop's elderly have it better than their counterparts throughout central Jersey's suburbs. They can at least speak their own language with each other, trading recipes and news from home.

Urged by her sons thousands of miles away, Harish's mother left Baroda because she felt so little was left for her there. She visits Harish and Kapila and Kajal regularly but rarely stays, because her health insurance is covered by Harish's wealthier brother in Hillsborough and because Harish's place is so small.

So small, Harish often thinks. So small yet so expensive. For what he pays in rent, he could live in one of the outer boroughs of New York City for as much; his apartment in Pennsylvania was less than half that. But affordable housing is scarce in the suburbs of New Jersey. And Hilltop knows that when one family leaves, another one will quickly take its place. In the process, places like Hilltop become virtual suburban ghettoes.

Although entrepreneurial Indians have thrived in the shadows of Hilltop, off the dollars and patronage of its residents, in businesses like groceries, video rentals, and laundromats, they tend to look down on those who live in the complex. Consider the reaction of a cashier at a nearby video store when asked if he lives in Hilltop. "No," he replies, taken aback. "Those people are different from us. Those of us with businesses live in our own houses."

Indeed, Hilltop represents the new problems suburbanites must contend with. There is a gang, known as the Punjabi Boyz, whose members spray their graffiti marks all over the brown buildings across the complex and squabble and fight with some of the Gujarati teenagers, usually over women. There are teens who smoke and drink and laugh and play their music loud at all hours, sometimes blaring it from open car doors. There are two liquor stores within walking distance, and both have cars regularly parked outside filled with desi youth. Inside the apartments, fights between couples can become so loud that walls shake, so loud the sound of slaps and tears and children's wails can be heard by the neighbors through the thin dividers. In Hilltop, as the Patel family learned the hard way, one person's business becomes everybody's business.

By the fall of 2000, though, Zankhana's marriage to a boy her parents didn't approve on that Christmas Eve nearly five years ago is old gossip. The neighborhood now loves Zankhana's baby, Simran, and has moved on to new sources of conversation. The family that lived diagonally across from the Patels moved away, for example. The man of the house held a master's degree but found himself working for a mailing company as a sorter at the age of fifty-one. When he arrived at Hilltop, he told neighbors that it would be temporary, that he would buy a house for his family. His seventeen-year-old daughter dropped out of school and went to work at a restaurant for $5 an hour, less than minimum wage. The family returned to India after less than three months in America.

Harish has seen so many like them pass through the Hilltop buildings that have been his home. He, too, dreams of returning, but for him going home isn't as easy as it once was. Home. Some days, Harish doesn't even know how to define it.

By October, it is clear Harish's employer is in trouble. He has seen the signs before. And he has been laid off before. If he can, this time, Harish would rather leave before being asked to. So he looks. Searching for work and worrying about money are almost second nature now.

He shows none of this doubt to Kapila and Kajal, however. "I will find a better job," he says over and over, almost often enough to believe it himself. He is the family jokester, making fun of Kapila's attempts to speak English, playing pranks on Kajal as though he, too, were a child. Then he switches gears into the disciplinarian, warning Kajal to keep her grades up, come home early, stay out of trouble.

By October 31, no new apartment has been found. Harish renews his lease for one year, paying $905 for the same one-bedroom with the stained walls, fraying carpet and ripped couches. When he first moved, it had been $600.

A few days later, the Patels exercise a right that will distinguish them from the people they were when they arrived in

America: the right to vote. They all became citizens just last year. To prepare for Election Day, Kapila and Kajal look to Harish for guidance. He is the only one in the family who occasionally reads the paper, admittedly only skimming the articles on his way to the classifieds. "I know the Democratic Party, so let's vote for Al Gore," he proclaims. "Eighty percent of Indians are Democrats."

"Bill Clinton did a lot of good," Kajal says in agreement.

So it is decided. In this, their first election in America, the Patels will vote Democratic. The morning of Election Day, Kajal drives her mother to their polling location and instructs her how to vote, American-style. Her mother is used to voting in India, where the process consisted of putting a ballot in a box. Because there was no national voter registration system for India's billion citizens, a black mark to show she had voted had been stamped onto Kapila's index fingernail, where it would remain for days.

"Just check off row number two, Ma," Kajal says in Gujarati.

Kapila obliges, then Kajal follows.

Harish doesn't vote until that night, after he gets home from his shift at Bradlees.

5

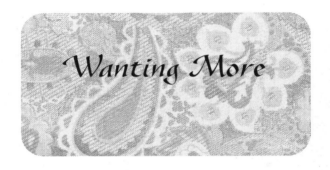

Wanting More

Election Day also distinguishes Pradip Kothari from the man he was when he first arrived in America. But for Pradip, Election Day signifies much more as well. It means an end to the phone calls from candidates seeking his support, his money, and his access to one of the wealthiest communities in America. After today, at least for a few months, they might remain silent.

"They call me when they need me," he laments. "Jai Hind, Namaste. They know a few words, but they're exploiting those words. There's no interest in appointing Indians." Only in getting their votes and money, Pradip says.

By the election of 2000, no New Jersey politician can afford to ignore the constituency Indians have become, and Pradip has been appointed, by himself and others, their spokesman. This season, as he has for the last few years of his ascent in the Indian community, Pradip attends their fund-raisers and meet-and-greets. Census figures are not out yet, but the survey taken in 1990 shows

Asian Indians' per capita income rolls in at $17,777, among immigrant groups trailing only the Japanese at $19,373.

Soon after he started getting involved again in politics, Pradip realized that where there was money, there would be politicians. He cons his daughters and their friends into attending functions by giving them $5 apiece. By now, after a decade of events, Nandini knows the ones where she's really needed and begs off most, citing her ever-crowded hospital work schedule. Her daughters have no such excuse.

"What are your plans for Friday night?" Pradip will ask.

"No plans yet," Payal or Toral will answer, hesitantly.

"Well, there's this fundraiser . . ."

Then Payal and Toral get on the phone to their friends: "Free dinner. Put on your suits."

During the dinners, inevitably Payal's mind wanders. She always wonders how Toral can sit there and listen, or at least *look* so attentive. This fall, they listened to Jon Corzine, the former head of Goldman Sachs, and Bob Franks, a Republican congressman. Neither especially impresses Pradip, but on Election Day he pulls the lever for Corzine. He does the same for Gore and for a whole host of local Democratic candidates. Voting Democrat has almost become force of habit for Pradip. He advises his family to do the same. Payal almost forgot there was even an election this morning, until her father reminded her to vote.

"Who should I vote for, Dad? Run those names by me again."

"Al Gore, Jon Corzine, you know, the Democrats. They do more for minorities."

Inwardly, he thinks his words might ring true on a national level. But the Democrats also were the ones who spent all those years tying him and his festival up in court. *On a local level, all politics is the same*, Pradip thinks to himself. Still, he tells Payal to vote a straight ticket.

As he votes, Pradip vows this will be his last year of being frustrated at Indians' lack of inclusion. "I'm going to play an active role in the upcoming election. I just need to find the right candidate."

Pradip's ascent to power among the block of merchants on Oak Tree Road had been a rapid one. After his window was broken in May 1990 and the police responded by telling him to call his insurance company, Pradip consulted his new neighbors and found they had been told the same thing. He concluded quickly that the police were a part of the problem. *Do they not see a pattern? Doesn't anyone find it curious that this prejudice is not just from the lower levels of people but all the way from top to bottom?* Pradip started to ask questions of the police department regarding its treatment of bias incidents. In the meantime, he befriended the growing number of Indian merchants who owned stores along Oak Tree Road.

A fast friend came in Chandrakant Patel, better known as Patel Senior, the owner of the restaurant Chowpatty, which had opened in August 1990. Patel had immigrated in 1987, more than a decade after Pradip, at the age of fifty-three with only a high school diploma. The eldest son in a traditional Gujarati family, he was left to take care of the family after his father's death in 1963. He gradually brought his brother and two sisters to the United States to work in his restaurants, catering business, and food manufacturing plant. Patel and Pradip quickly joined forces to lobby the township to patrol the area with more police cars. "Don't you think it's a coincidence that *only* the Indian shops have their windows broken?" Pradip asked. But since rents were cheap, Indian entrepreneurs kept setting up shop.

Heightened police presence soon became a double-edged sword. While they kept the vandals away, the police also issued tickets to cars as though their quota for the month had suddenly doubled. Some were legitimate, given to double-parked cars or vehicles near hydrants. Others seemed inane, for cars parked six and a half inches from the curb rather than six. The township, meanwhile, wanted to adopt an ordinance restricting parking in the area to residents. Pradip again questioned township officials on their seemingly arbitrary decisions and got himself appointed to the Human Relations Commission.

Through his position on the commission, Pradip started to form alliances with other minority groups. In the process, he learned about the civil rights movement of the 1960s, relating that history of collective protest and action to the example his parents had set for him and his days as a student organizer. Before gatherings of Indians, Pradip would frequently chastise them. "Some of our people are bigots, and it's uncalled for. We feel superior. But why?" Then he would ask this question until it became almost a refrain: "Those who were here before us—African Americans, Jews, Latinos—has their struggle for civil rights not benefited us?"

Relations between blacks and Asian immigrants have historically been classified as tense, often fueled by references to Asians as a "model minority." Inevitably such a designation puts down other minority groups, leading to divisive racial relations and a tendency for Asians to categorize themselves alongside whites versus blacks or Latinos. In his book *The Karma of Brown Folk,* scholar Vijay Prashad borrows W.E.B. Du Bois's question to black America—"How does it feel to be a problem?"—and asks his fellow desis: "How does it feel to be a solution?" Prashad concludes that the success of Asians in the United States has to do not with race or ethnicity but with the selection of highly educated, highly skilled workers for immigration. He claims the very term "model minority" has been deployed as "a weapon in the war against black America." Further, Prashad asserts that prominent Indians such as Deepak Chopra, the renowned spiritual guru, have only served to further exoticize India's people and traditions within the confines of American culture and that Indians need to align themselves with racial minorities more closely if they seek any political voice or influence.

It's a message similar to the one Pradip invokes. Realistically, though, Pradip is often the first to say that unifying Indians among themselves—let alone with other racial minorities—is the toughest of tasks.

In July 1990, an organizer from the India Day Parade in New York came into Quick Travel and asked if Pradip was interested in putting together a float for the annual parade along Madison Avenue commemorating India's independence.

"Sure," Pradip said.

"Really?" the organizer asked.

"We can put *something* together. Why do you seem so surprised?"

"I've asked the people around here before, and nobody ever wants to do it."

This year would be different, Pradip assured him. And it was. Galvanized by broken eggs and windows, the merchants along Oak Tree Road contributed to the effort led by Pradip, hanging banners off two floats with their business names on them. In the parade which often featured floats from India's individual states—from Gujarat to Himachal Pradesh to Maharastra—Pradip was proud of the unity Oak Tree Road showed that year.

That fall, Pradip was approached to help organize a Navratri at the local middle school. The event sold out, so the following year a bigger venue was sought. That, too, proved too small. So Pradip sought something bigger. And so his involvement went. He formed the Indo-American Cultural Society and gradually became the first source reporters turned to for comment on the area's growing Indian community. For most of the 1990s, Pradip spent much of his time fighting the lawsuit filed by the township demanding a curfew be set on Navratri. His group ultimately prevailed, when a judge ruled the curfew an imposition on the group's right to assemble. But the years Pradip spent in and out of courtrooms and lawyers' offices left their toll. The township recruited former associates of Pradip's to criticize his leadership style, to chastise his celebrations as too ostentatious and borderline sacrilegious, to question where Navratri's funds went. The phrase "divide and conquer" had never meant so much to Pradip.

A part of it was the community's own doing. Every year the listings of events related to Navratri showed at least two competing functions and organizations. Consider this listing from 1997:

> 1997 Navratri Ramzat. Garba and Dandia Raas with prominent Bombay Dhamaka Group. Organized by Indo-American Cultural Association. Venue: J. P. Stevens High School, Grove Ave., Edison, NJ. Time: Oct. 3, 4, 10, 11 from 8 p.m. Contact: Natu Patel (908) 769–9006.
>
> Navratri '97. Edison turns as 8th annual Navratri returns. Featuring Bombay's best group and surprise Bollywood celebrities. Organized by Indo-American Cultural Society. Venue: Raritan Center, Edison, NJ. Time: Oct, 3, 4, 10, 11, 17, 18, 24, 25 from 9 p.m. Contact: Pradip Kothari (908) 283–9696.

The former was Pradip's onetime rival Prabhu Patel's group, although by the time of these ads he and Pradip were exchanging pleasantries at Indian events. While definite camps had been formed, there was no question who carried more influence. Pradip was the one everyone, from media to politicians to wannabe activists, turned to for the Indian voice.

This history is the one Pradip takes into the voting booth with him on Election Day of 2000. The census this year will show that one out of every ten Middlesex County residents is Asian, more likely to be from India than any other country. Yet the county's ballot has not a single Asian name. Pradip knows the political players. Some people even say he's one of them. But as he pulls the levers, it sure doesn't feel that way.

6

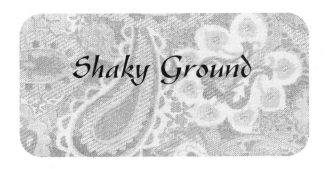

Shaky Ground

Lipi has a ritual she follows every morning. She turns on her computer at work and reads the websites of the *Times of India,* the *Assam Tribune,* the *Hindu.* She does this before she logs on to more local papers like the *Star-Ledger* or the *New York Times,* before she reads of what's going on in her own backyard. Somehow it just feels right to start the day off reading of her former home.

Lipi's upbringing as the daughter of a mining engineer for India's Oil and Natural Gas Corporation took her all over India. Her education took place in dozens of central government schools, known as India's "great equalizer" for their ability to bring together children of different regions, religions, castes, and economic backgrounds to study. But even at an early age, Lipi was struck by how some parts of Indian society moved full speed ahead while others hindered progress. When she was seven years old, her family lived in Silchar, an area of Assam dominated by Bengalis, in a subsidized housing complex for government employees. On each side of her house's road ran streams of water carrying away sewage and waste. "One side of the street used to throw their garbage on the other side and our side used to throw it on theirs," Lipi recalls years later when asked why she left. "You cannot romanticize India. It's a vicious circle. It's a paradox."

No matter how far from Assam, her parents attempted to retain the family's ties to the region by speaking Assamese in the home and bringing in a language tutor to teach their three children to read and write in their native tongue. Despite her need to follow her husband's various postings, Lipi's mother usually worked as a teacher and encouraged her daughters to pursue careers in whatever they desired. Lipi's sister went on to become a doctor, while Lipi gravitated toward engineering. She returned to the northeast to attend Assam Engineering College in Guwahati. Despite the progress women had made in India, Lipi was still one of only a handful enrolled in the program. "All the boys always know the girls because there's so few," she says. She was known among the engineering boys for her biting tongue and refusal to put up with their flirtation, known colloquially as "proposals" among students.

Again and again, Lipi would find herself the only girl. In her first job, at Schlumberger, the company had to have a tailor and a shoemaker make a special set of construction overalls and boots for her petite frame. When she had transferred to Lucent in August 2000, she found very few women in her group. By now, she hardly sees it as an issue, and it rarely is. She's good at what she does, and the guys come to her for help. Her position entails writing software for Lucent's voiceover Internet protocol, a cheaper alternative to telephone networks.

When Lipi arrives, Lucent ranks among New Jersey's largest employers, the product of a massive telecommunications overhaul in the early 1990s. In 1996, telecom giant AT&T spun off its systems and technology unit to create Lucent Technologies. By the time the spinoff was completed, Lucent had plans to shed its phone-company culture and embrace the entrepreneurial spirit of Bell Labs, a former AT&T business unit it incorporated. In 1927, Bell Labs provided the first demonstration of television in the United States. It would go on to produce eleven Nobel Prize winners. To work at Bell Labs provided scientists some protection from the corporate world of quarterly earnings and dividends, profits and bottom lines.

Much of that changed when Bell Labs became absorbed into Lucent. Lucent executives decided they could not afford to stand by and watch the venture capital and IPO market take off. "We wanted to emulate the Silicon Valley model inside Lucent," said one Lucent partner.

The company also emulated Silicon Valley's bust. Lucent's first-quarter earnings in 2000 had fallen short of analysts' expectations by almost a third. Its stock price began the first signs of steady decline since the company was spun off.

For Lipi, her job at Lucent allows for much more creativity than the one she had at AT&T. Not that that's saying much. The job's a grind, perhaps explaining why some dub H-1B visa holders "high-tech coolies." Because H-1B's cannot be easily promoted, there is little of the rat race Lipi remembers from her time in India. India, ironically, felt more competitive. "You would never see any dumbos out there," she says, referring to her old office in Bombay. "Either you're a good developer or not. There's a lot of mediocrity here. In India, there's no place for it."

Her words debunk the notion that only India's "best and brightest" make it to the United States. With the growth of certification courses in India, everybody, it seems, can be a software developer, or a computer programmer. Across India's metropolitan areas, billboards and signs for technical institutes and training programs posted on poles abound. They ask, "Why do it in the U.S. when you can do it in Bangalore?" or proclaim the opposite, "Learn JAVA: Guaranteed Jobs Abroad."

In Bombay, one building next to a McDonald's in the city's Andheri West section boasts so many information technology signs that they drown each other's message out. "Here, that's all that's in demand," one seventeen-year-old student spending her summer vacation taking courses in computer programming explains.

When companies in the States needed workers to fill the positions created by the U.S. tech boom, India was more than willing to provide. The offers came steadily through the late 1990s and into early 2000. But as Lucent shows Lipi this fall, the good times might not last.

The company already has begun spinning off its microelectronics unit, a maker of optical components and semiconductors, to focus more on the business of making equipment for data, wireless, and fiber-optic networks. Meanwhile, the stock continues to take a beating.

Still, in October, Sanku and Lipi take $500 out of their savings account and put it in Lucent stock—not much, but their first investment in the market since they immigrated. In choosing Lucent, they are putting their money into one of the most widely owned stocks in America. Never considering themselves financially savvy, the Sarmas say they have a history of watching others make and lose millions and prefer to play it safe. "I don't want to be a pauper," says Lipi, "but I don't want to be a millionaire either." In Bombay, the city housing India's stock exchanges and the country's financial capital, Sanku had lost all the money he invested. Lipi used to chide him that Gujarati teenagers seemed to have the system figured out better than he. In Bombay, they never had much money left over after paying their expenses, so sending money to their families wasn't even an option. Now they send traveler's checks worth about $200 to Sanku's parents monthly and occasionally to Lipi's. Sometimes, Lipi wonders if they need to belt-tighten at all, but feels there's no need for alarm yet.

By early November, she changes her mind. On November 9, Lucent announces it plans to eliminate as many as 10,000 jobs, 10 percent of its workforce. In late December, irate shareholders sue Lucent, claiming the company reported inflated earnings estimates for the fourth quarter. Its stock price plummets, in a market already reeling from the uncertainty of who the next president will be.

Each day, Lipi goes to work wondering if she might be next. Her supervisor assures her the layoffs affect upper management, but Lipi can't be sure.

On the phone to her father in India, Lipi tells him about her sudden loss of job security. She tries to explain what layoffs are, with little luck. It dawns on her that India, despite its overpopulated, impoverished status, offers a certain class of people a stability that suddenly seems to have disappeared from her and Sanku's lives. In India, there's a shameful stigma attached to job loss. "You can stay there forever in one job," she says. "Laying off is still pretty rare. Changing jobs is rare. Here, it's not like if you were fired, it's a discredit to the person. It's totally different."

On New Year's Eve, Sanku and Lipi travel to an Assamese family's home in Wyckoff, a town in northern New Jersey, for a party. They join about thirty Assamese immigrants for a night of songs and dancing and drinking. Lipi wears a sequined silver blouse. She and Sanku and Siku shake their shoulders in sync to bhangra, upbeat Punjabi dance music, and sway and twirl to the beat of Top 40. Later on, Sanku sings the songs of home in Hindi and Assamese as the ever-drunker crowd eggs him on, saying, "Aru eta, aru eta," or "One more, one more." He obliges with a ghazal, "Naye ghare ke paani se," a duet he sings with Lipi about longing for one's beloved. "I smell the water from the earthen pitcher, I am reminded of your fragrance," goes the first line.

They return to their offices to begin a new year filled with uncertainty. Lucent starts off the first month of the year with the announcement that it will eliminate 10,000 more jobs and shut down a factory in the Midwest with another 6,000 workers. For Lipi, the signs are clear that the America that welcomed her family with a limousine ride is becoming a different place. She used to receive phone calls every day from recruiters for body shops across the country asking her if she was looking for another job. She never understood how they got her résumé.

The phone calls don't come anymore.

7

Destructive Times

The day after a Christmas season that can't save it, Bradlees files for Chapter 11 bankruptcy protection. Harish's manager calls a meeting at 10:00 A.M. to give them the news they already know: this time, there will be no saving the company. All 105 Bradlees stores will shut down, and more than 10,000 employees will lose their jobs. Thirty stores are to close in New Jersey, affecting more than a quarter of Bradlees entire workforce, 2,600 people. Unlike most of the workers in the 584,000-square-foot distribution facility where Harish works, he will be keeping his job for a few more days.

Because Harish's job involves reconciling vendors' bills, he is needed to settle outstanding accounts. He reports to work the day after the layoff announcement, unsure of whether it will be his last. It's an eerie feeling to be among the few survivors of a layoff, to look around and not see the familiar colleagues. Yet it's a feeling Harish is all too familiar with in this stage of his career. Because it's December, Harish knows that no one will be looking for new workers. Not until January will there be Help Wanted ads in the classifieds again, not until then will budgets allow for new hires, not until then will the people cashing out after bonuses make their exit. Harish has learned this much from his years in America.

The end comes right before New Year's Eve. On Friday, December 29, Harish is informed he'll get one week of salary for every year worked. *Great*, he thinks. *I've only been here a year and a half.*

By January, he's collecting unemployment, only 60 percent of the total he's used to. Unlike the layoff at First Fidelity in 1994 in which Harish had been a casualty, Bradlees employees don't get a career center or human resources hot line. "No phone numbers, no help in finding another job, no party, no nothing," Harish says.

And no second income. Kapila hasn't been reporting to work, collecting a reduced salary in disability. A diabetic who takes pills in the morning and an injection at night, she had an infected foot that was misdiagnosed by a doctor the first time around. Kapila's latest ailment confines her to the couch to watch television she doesn't completely understand. She's been complaining of a stiff arm, too, and has difficulty moving it.

Once again, Harish finds himself in hard times and doesn't know where to turn. There's no escape, not to India, not to Pennsylvania. He's learned so many times that moving to a new place won't guarantee he can find a new job. One day, Harish knows, he will go back. "I don't want to die here," he says. "I will die in India." But at age fifty-four, it is not yet time to plan for such matters.

India wasn't always home. In 1957, when Harish was ten, his father moved to Uganda to work as a private contractor. This was a growing trend in the late nineteenth and early twentieth centuries among Gujarati families lured by a plethora of jobs constructing a railroad system. Many stayed, setting up small businesses, operating on low profit margins, living cheaply. In *Migrations and Cultures,* Thomas Sowell observes, "the Indians . . .

worked long hours under what would be impossible conditions for Europeans." Their economic impact, he goes on to say, was enormous. "The economic role of the Indians in Uganda can perhaps best be appreciated by considering what happened after they left. The economy collapsed."

The Patels lived in Soroti for one year, then moved to the capital, Kampala. They had a servant, a Ugandan man who polished Harish's shoes and ironed his uniform before he went to school every morning. The young boy helped his mother with the cleaning and cooking. "It was a very good time for Indians," Harish recalls. "All the black people were working for us."

In 1962, his grandfather died. With nobody else to run the family farm, Harish's father followed his duty as the eldest son and returned to his Gujurat, turning his back on a land where he had been able to afford private school for his sons, a servant, and a business he had built on his own.

Thus Harish grew up knowing how prosperity can quickly enter and exit one's life. During these tough times, he pronounces the period a sign of Kaliyug, a period of destruction in Hinduism, voicing his faith that vicissitudes are cyclical.

It's almost as if the earthquake clinches this belief.

8

Standing Room Only

Pradip Kothari's daughters are often known as just that: Pradip Kothari's daughters. As he returned to taking up causes, increasingly Payal and Toral grew up outside his limelight. Before Navratri, friends would inevitably come out of the woodwork, then casually ask for free tickets or an opportunity to schmooze with the stars from Bollywood, India's movie industry, flown in for the festivals. Payal and Toral, rarely seen with their parents except during aarti, would hop onstage and deliver the bouquets of flowers to Bollywood legends like Amitabh Bachchan and Madhuri Dixit. Whereas Indian teens would likely kill for such opportunity, neither Payal nor Toral's adolescent face showed any awe. The problem was, they rarely watched the movies these actors were in.

That changed as they grew into bona fide desi teenagers who danced and shook their shoulders to bhangra. Desi teens have appropriated the Punjabi music and dance as a symbol of their hybrid identities, mixing it with rap, reggae, and hip hop. One popular remix, originated in the United Kingdom, blends a bhangra beat with the tune from the *Knight Rider* theme song. Payal and Toral had friends who grew obsessed with Bollywood, but for the sisters the movies, dismissed as "cheesy" by both of them, served a more utilitarian purpose: they watched Bollywood films to learn steps to the dances they performed at fashion shows, community functions, and even an annual "Bhangra Blowout" in Washington, D.C. Events such as Bhangra Blowout have become incredibly competitive as college-age students try to outperform each other, aided by colorful costumes blending East and West, stunts more reminiscent of acrobatics than dance moves, and background music that combines Bollywood, Hollywood, and all points in between.

By December, Payal feels she's back in control of her life. She ends her first semester at Kean with a 3.8 grade point average, especially enjoying a class on cultures of the world that forced her to write about her surroundings. "I learned to go up to the professor and say, 'How can I improve?' "

Armed with an A in a hard biology class, Payal tunes in to *ER* each Thursday night and yells to her parents and sister, "I *know* what those terms mean!" Someone at school has told her she could earn $75,000 as a health care administrator. "I'm all into it now," she says.

Toral focuses on the short-term future. College rejections in April, or, dare she wish it, acceptances? Prom in May. A speech in June—it's official; Toral is Colonia High School's salutatorian for the class of 2001. She shares the spot with a Chinese American girl who in the beginning Toral thought might edge her out. No matter; they ended up having the same GPA. For the next few months, though, there is only a winter of waiting, a season Toral shares with anxious, ambitious high school students across the country.

The success of ABCDs—American Born Confused Desis—such as Toral demonstrates the mark the children of immigrants have made on suburban school districts. Asian immigrants, the so-called model minority, were lauded for the success they had achieved professionally and academically in a relatively short amount of time until a newly sensitized population ceased using the backhand compliment. In central New Jersey, though, school administrators and teachers will go so far as to say the influx of Indian students was the best thing that could have happened to their districts.

By the time the first wave of Indian immigrants arrived, Middlesex County already exemplified New Jersey's postwar school-building boom. Until 1954, children in Edison attended regional schools in the neighboring communities of Metuchen, Highland Park, Rahway, Perth Amboy, and Woodbridge. By the 1950s, young families, helped by the GI Bill and driven by the need to escape the congestion and high rents of Manhattan, were flocking to the suburbs of New Jersey. "It became apparent that a high school would have to be constructed within Edison to accommodate the educational needs of a growing, youthful population," writes David Sheehan in his book about Edison, *Welcome to Edison: An Enlightened Community*. The 1954 groundbreaking for Edison High School would soon be followed by another across town, named after the president of the Board of Education, J. P Stevens Jr. It wasn't until the late 1970s that the list of graduates started to include names like Patel and Shah. Quickly, these names filled the top spots when class rank came out.

"They made me look good as a principal," says Cedric Richardson, who served as principal of Stevens for several years. "In 1993, of the 138 students in the National Honor Society, 92 were Indian or Asian."

Later arrivals, however, faced resentment of their success and of their high numbers. "They smell, I don't want to sit next to them," mimics Richardson, echoing a stereotype he'd often heard in the hallways of his school. Ironically, he says the children of Toral's generation—the ABCDs—looked down on those who came after them. "The first wave and professional families seemed embarrassed by the second wave," Richardson observes.

The school districts were among the few places township officials could turn to get a handle on just how many South Asian newcomers filled their towns. Each year, schools submitted data for the New Jersey School Report Card on everything from attendance to test scores. The third item on the list was language diversity.

In 2000, when Toral entered her senior year at Colonia High School, 2 percent of the students spoke Gujarati at home. The same numbers spoke Urdu and Polish. Eighty-one percent spoke English. But the same figures for the comparable period at Stevens and Edison high schools tell a different story. At Edison High, 6 percent of students hailed from a home where Gujarati was primarily spoken, the same number as its Spanish speakers. Three percent came from Urdu-speaking households, 2 percent from Hindi-speaking ones. English was still the language of choice in a significant majority of households, 65 percent.

That was not the case at Stevens. Just under half of the student body could say it lived in a home where English was the primary language. The next largest group, 14 percent, went from school to a home where Gujarati was spoken, presumably a home where spongy yellow dhokla was served and after-school greetings consisted of "Kem cho?" Eight percent of the students' households spoke Mandarin, while 4 percent of them spoke Hindi. Korean, Cantonese, and Russian came in at 3 percent apiece. Those numbers showed that at least seventeen of every hundred Stevens students were South Asian. Thus it was entirely likely that an Indian or two was in every class.

Yet in the nearby schools Toral and Payal attended, they remained among a handful of Indians. The people they socialized with on the weekends were the children of their parents' friends or teens encountered at desi parties or Navratri. Few, if any, of their friends were recent arrivals, dubbed by some sociologists the "1.5 generation." The girls included their parents' generation in their low tolerance for "not having a clue." At family dinner parties, Toral cringed when "aunties" and "uncles" would say, "Do you remember me? Do you remember we carried you when you were five days old?" Counting on her ability to turn up her perfect pink lips into an all-purpose response, Toral inwardly thought, *Why would anyone retain memory as an infant?*

In mid-January, Payal and Toral travel across the country for perhaps the most famous of parties among desi youth. The annual South Asian Student Alliance, or SASA, attracts Indian student associations from colleges across the country for a weekend of seminars, panels, and, the biggest draw, parties. At SASA conventions, organizers have such a hard time getting people out of bed after a night of partying that they make attendance at at least two panels a prerequisite for attending the parties. In 2001, SASA is being held in San Francisco, a city surrounded by suburbs also marked by immigrant arrivals, notably Indians. But the conference Payal and Toral attend stresses the need for Indians to move beyond careers in engineering or medicine.

Payal and Toral's memories of the event, though, would not be of their career-building. Nor of the remarks made by author Chitra Banerjee Divakaruni or Vinod Dham, credited with being the force behind Intel's original Pentium chip, or Rajat Gupta, managing director of McKinsey & Co. Rather, the teenagers from New Jersey take advantage of being away from home to, in Payal's words, "go out together and not care what people thought about us . . . the 'he said–she said' drama that consumes every adolescent life."

Several days later, as Payal sleeps in her downstairs bedroom, the phone rings in the Kothari household. It's 5:00 A.M. on January 26. As the years go by, Indians living in America dread middle-of-the-night phone calls; they can only mean bad news from home or a relative who miscalculated the time difference. Pradip prays for the latter as he answers.

It's his brother calling from Ohio. There has been an earthquake in Gujarat, a deadly one, possibly the worst India has ever seen. He hasn't been able to reach their parents, Ramanlal and Sumati, in Baroda.

Ironically, Pradip is scheduled to be on a flight to Baroda this very night. Ramanlal requires knee surgery, and his children are taking turns flying to India to take care of him. Most ninety-year-olds would have just accepted the weak knee, but not Ramanlal. He and Sumati had been driving their car through the congested streets of Baroda—no small feat for even the driving professional, dodging potholes and pedestrians, cows and scooters—until last year, when their children forced them to stop, chipping in for a full-time driver. Because his health is so good otherwise, doctors say Ramanlal can go ahead with the surgery.

In the early hours of this Friday morning, details on the quake are sketchy. The quake registered a magnitude of 7.9 on the Richter scale. It shook the earth for more than 1,200 miles around, hitting Gujarat hardest. Thousands, perhaps tens of thousands, are dead.

For four hours, Pradip tries to call Baroda. Finally, around 9:00 A.M., he gets through and learns everyone is fine. Shaken up, they tell him they definitely felt the tremor. In the meantime, the Associated Press is calling; so is NBC, ABC, the *Star-Ledger.* Does Mr. Kothari have any comment?

"At this moment, we are trying to figure out what we can do and what we should do," he is quoted as saying over and over.

Payal hears the phone ring again and again but doesn't answer, relishing the fact that she can sleep in on classless Fridays. When she finally wakes and heads into the family's living room, taking her seat on the edge of the pink leather couch, Pradip asks her to put the TV on channel 33, CNN.

"Why? What's going on?" she asks.

"There was an earthquake in Gujarat."

"Oh my God, that's so scary. Are Dada and Dadi okay?"

Payal remains glued to the television for the rest of the day, while Pradip readies for his evening flight. He fields calls from the media and members of the Indo-American Cultural Society on his cellular phone until boarding time. When Payal logs on to her e-mail account, the forwards have already started. Devastating photos of the disaster—a child crying by a bleeding woman, presumably his mother. Addresses of where to send donations. Pledges to donate proceeds from that weekend's desi parties to earthquake relief.

Meanwhile, the efforts to mobilize Edison's large Gujarati community are also under way. In their tendency to group themselves regionally, as Gujaratis, as Bengalis, as Punjabis, and so on, Indian immigrants mirrored previous arrivals, such as the Irish and Germans who often divided themselves into Catholic and Protestant camps. Yet his community's gumption is both a source of pride and annoyance to Pradip. *The more an Indian sets himself apart, the more he is acting in self-interest.* "Our cause is diluted because of our own people's attitude. 'What is there for me?' they ask, rather than 'What is there for all of us?'" Pradip says many times. "They should think not as Punjabi but as people from the Indian subcontinent and a minority."

Indeed, the aftermath of the Gujarat earthquake demonstrates bonds various Indian groups in America forged with each other. Pradip surely would have been proud of the scene the weekend after the quake at Royal Albert's Palace, indeed a palatial structure that rises unexpectedly from the middle of one of the last woodsy areas left in Central Jersey. The heads of major Indian organizations have gathered to brainstorm how they can channel their efforts to help. If Pradip is the "Godfather," these men—and they are mostly men—are his henchmen. Pradip, noticeably absent, checks in from Gujarat by calling Chowpatty owner Chandrakant Patel's cellular phone. The meeting includes several

Gujarati organizations but also pan-Indian groups such as the Federation of Indian Associations and the Association of Indians in America, and regional groups from Maharastra and Punjab.

There is H. R. Shah, who built an empire out of Krauszer's, the convenience store chain, and then went on to buy TV Asia, a channel devoted to programming about desis. When the tall, wiry, graying Shah arrives at the meeting, a half hour late on the clock but punctual on Indian Standard Time, three men get up to offer him their seats. Shah admittedly is most comfortable speaking in Gujarati. But before the crowd of two hundred, he musters in English, "What happened is an earthquake happened. Many people died in this things."

There is Kiran Desai, the appointed chairman of Old Bridge Township's zoning board, a loyal Democrat and a man who sought elected office in politics but has been branded by local officials as "not ready." Under the lights of the banquet room, standing against a wall where a U.S. flag crisscrosses an Indian one, Desai warns that the money raised should not go to any government agency. With the knowledge that corruption in Indian government is the norm, not the exception, members of the audience nod in agreement. The president of the Indian Cultural Association of Central New Jersey, Veena Agarwala, one of the few women in the room, stands to raise issues none of the men had. "Many children are also looking for ways to help," she says. "And what about the mental health of the people here who lost family?"

Also central to relief efforts is a pink temple erected off Woodbridge Avenue in Edison out of an old toy factory. The temple is one of twenty in the United States funded by a religious organization headquartered in Ahmedabad, Bochasanwasi Shree Aksharpurushottam Sanstha, known simply as BAPS. On February 4, the week after the earthquake, its parking lot is filled with Camrys and Accords—the stereotypical desi cars of choice for affordability and reliability—with BAPS relief stickers, fliers, and flags affixed to them. The women start to greet one another in clusters, slipping their shoes off and storing them in wooden shelves in a room outside the temple area.

The service, scheduled to begin at 4:00 P.M., definitely operates on IST. One man vacuums the red carpet of the interior, where just a handful of men and woman sit cross-legged. At this temple, men sit in the front of the room, while women sit behind. BAPS volunteer Trusha Patel, of Edison, says worshipers' minds "must be pure as they pray, not thinking about the opposite sex."

BAPS's North American operations are headquartered in Edison. As worshipers kneel before framed photos of various deities, their children mimic their movements. At the end of a prayer, one man stretches his body out flat on the floor, only to have his son climb on top as if to play horsie. The father continues praying, unfazed. Behind him comes a man who moments before had been a parking lot attendant. Rolling up his orange apron, he kneels and becomes just another worshiper.

By 5:00 P.M. the temple's floor is filled with crossed legs, half the bare feet tucked modestly under saris. The elderly sit on folding chairs, cognizant of their weak joints. And the reports from community leaders once again begin. Some kids between the ages of seven and eleven who had stood outside a Pathmark in Edison had collected $1,000 in change over four hours. Another group of kids hit the Middlesex Mall and solicited $2,000. Then the hall silences, remaining quiet as images of the devastation and the dead flicker before them on a screen. Women shed tears, dabbing tears with the dupattas of their salwar kameezes or the tails of their saris, while men clear throats.

A somber procession of politicians follows, led by Edison mayor George Spadoro and U.S. Senator Robert Torricelli. Spadoro, who traveled to India with President Clinton in 2000, reminds the crowd that Baroda has a sister city in Edison. "We have a personal interest here," he says.

Torricelli follows by invoking his own Italian immigrant heritage. "Your fellow Americans feel your pain. This community is an important part of Edison and New Jersey, but the U.S. community, too. You want more than our prayers. The challenge is next month and next year. Housing is not rebuilt in a month. Next year I will remain involved when others forget, but I ask the same of you. The fact that you are here tonight says much about the type of people you are. You did not turn your back on your country. You did not forget."

As the congregation applauds, Pradip remains in Gujarat surveying the devastation firsthand. He meets with Indian politicians such as Gujarat's chief minister (equivalent to a U.S. governor) and chooses to forgo flying home early for the gathering at the temple. There, his name is invoked by none other than Praful Raja, an ally of Prabhu Patel's, who admits Pradip is not a man he has gotten along with but says he deserves thanks for checking in from Gujarat to make sure the community reached out to politicians for their help.

Pradip and Nandini often say they have problems with the way the Hindu temples in New Jersey are run. Nandini, specifically, objects to the separation of men and women and to the use of a religious gathering place as one to showcase clothing and jewelry. Pradip, despite the religious nature of the festival he organizes every year, considers himself quite secular; he couldn't explain the significance of Navratri to a *New York Times* reporter when asked in 1997.

"BAPS is trying to be a political player," he says. "They are loaded with volunteers and money; they don't need money. They always bring a politician in there. Outsiders get very impressed with it. But they do nothing for our community here."

Pradip voices these thoughts after two weeks spent in his homeland in the quake's aftermath. On the evening of March 20, 2001, his office door is closed—rare for Pradip. Bhailal, his assistant and office manager and arguably the one who keeps the business afloat while Pradip takes on more causes, fields the flurry of phone calls before closing business for the day.

The voices in the room continue to escalate, then subdue into deep discussion. Finally, at 9:15, out comes Pradip, right on the IST he so hates, for another meeting. With him is John Vrtaric, a tall blondish man with a Polish accent who extols Pradip's virtues for a good ten minutes.

"I've known him since 1983," Vrtaric says. "Whenever I ask Peter why he got involved, he says, ''Cuz I didn't want any more broken windows.' "

He bursts into laughter and says to Pradip: "Peter, think about it."

Pradip nods as Vrtaric leaves. "The next couple of years will be important," he says. "I'm not seeing any possibilities in Middlesex County from the Democratic Party. There's no room for anyone. It's like an incumbent line every time. The Republican Party is in disarray."

Yet the party is seeking freeholder candidates for Middlesex County and has asked Pradip for some names. He can't come up with any.

Only a few months after he voted for a series of Democrats, Pradip tears into them.

"We keep getting lip service from the Democrats, and we've been supporting them for many years. Only Frank Pallone gives us serious thought." Pallone, a Democratic congressman since 1988, is a founding member of the India Caucus in Washington, spurred by a constituency he noticed was increasingly South Asian. He made the discovery before many of his fellow politicians in New Jersey and is frequently quoted in the ethnic Indian publications on issues facing both the subcontinent and its diaspora.

"Democrat, Republican, I don't think it matters," says Pradip. "We need to get individually involved and play an active role in politics."

A week later, on March 26, Pradip starts to call reporters he's befriended over the years.

"Peter Kothari here. I've decided to run on the Republican Party for freeholder."

On March 29, 2001, Pradip announces his candidacy more officially at the county GOP convention held at the Pines Manor banquet hall in Edison. John Vrtaric stands by his side for much of the night. To anyone who will listen, Vrtaric stops to tell the story of how he convinced Pradip to run.

On the night of the annual Republican convention, the Indians who come to support Pradip stand mostly in the back of the room, observing the hundreds seated before them decked in elephant gear and American flags. Many of these Indians are not even from Middlesex County. Mercer County resident Smita Patel drove forty-five minutes from Princeton Junction to support her friend Pete. Shailesh Vyas passes out business cards with his Ahmedabad garment factory's address. Vyas, not a citizen, not even a permanent resident, just a visitor to the United States, says he simply wants to show a fellow Indian his support.

For many of Pradip's supporters, tonight is their first venture into politics. It turns into a night of firsts. That night, Pradip (Peter) Kothari, as his name will appear on campaign literature and ultimately the ballot, becomes the first Asian American to run for a countywide seat in the county with the highest number of New Jersey's Asians.

An entourage surrounds Pradip all night long. He has gotten a new haircut and even clipped the few hairs that usually grace his ears. In an evening filled with at least a dozen candidates announcing their bids for office, Pradip is the clear star.

Payal has a night class at Kean and can't make it. Toral and Nandini stay at a distance.

"I'm happy for him," Nandini says carefully, watching her words to reporters. She wears a gray suit and black heels, a departure from the Indian outfits she usually dons to accompany

Pradip. "It means more work, though." She sighs. After all, this is the role she has played to Pradip before.

As his nomination is announced, Pradip stands at the back of the room giving an interview to TV Asia, one of several ethnic media outlets covering the event. Twice, his name booms from the announcer's microphone. Visibly nervous and gripping an acceptance speech, Pradip politely excuses himself and walks briskly to the front of the room.

The other two candidates, Woodbridge resident Joseph Paone and former South River councilwoman Tina Martins Cruz, had already been nominated and accepted less than a half hour into the event. Quickly, it becomes clear that Kothari's process will be different. His nominator, Assemblyman Sam Thompson, takes the crowd back to 1492.

"Our country was discovered by a brave man sailing for the seas of India," he says, referring to Christopher Columbus. "Were it not for India, we might not be here today."

Eventually, Thompson, a graying man who represents Middlesex County in the New Jersey legislature, brings the crowd to modern-day America. Asian immigrants comprise 13.9 percent of Middlesex County's 900,000 people, the largest minority group, he tells them. And just in case this audience doesn't understand the significance of numbers, Thompson mentions his own doctor is Indian, as is his wife's. Dr. Patel and Dr. Chaudery.

Then comes the kicker, the reason Pradip is the star: "We send a message to all minorities. This is the party of opportunity and we welcome you."

Political experts later translate Thompson's words to mean the GOP needs to change in order to survive in New Jersey.

"Both parties in New Jersey are dominated by white males," John Weingart, associate director of the Eagleton Institute of Politics at Rutgers University, says a couple of days later. "The Census is confirming that the racial and ethnic composition has changed pretty dramatically. There are groups with ethnic heritages that have not been represented in politics. There are sizable populations that have the potential to vote in fairly high numbers."

Yet in Middlesex County, it wasn't for lack of trying that Asians had not been able to snag a single one of the hundreds of elected seats throughout the county and its twenty-five municipalities. In 1999, the GOP backed Baljit (Bill) Singh and Andrew Wu for Edison council positions. They lost, each receiving almost half the votes of the four Democratic winners. GOP leaders later said it was like pulling teeth to get the two to campaign; most watchers say a Republican running in the county does so with cards stacked against him anyway. In Old Bridge Township, Kiran Desai once expressed interest in running for the township council but was passed over for a better-known candidate. Desai, still a loyal Democrat, says he agreed with the decision. "My daughter, my son, my niece, they will have a chance to run for general election," says Desai, who was appointed chairman of the zoning board as a consolation prize of sorts. "They are still not ready for us."

Tonight this crowd, though, appears ready for Peter, as they call him. Despite his close alliances with Democrats over the years (Woodbridge mayor Jim McGreevey spent four hours in Pradip's travel agency on the Sunday before the convention to persuade him not to run), they see a glimmer in this minority candidate. If he could really pull in all the Asian voters, did the GOP perhaps have a chance in the county?

Before they allow Pradip to speak, GOP brass extol his leadership and virtue, waxing poetic as they have for no other candidate this night. "He came here to pursue the American Dream, to have freedom," says one.

"He'll bring energy and enthusiasm to the freeholder board," promises Jesal Amin, who seconds Pradip's candidacy and is to serve as his campaign manager.

As Pradip steps forward, the cameraman from TV Asia focuses not on him but on the clapping and cheering audience.

Pradip steps to the microphone. The cameraman pivots to zoom in on the candidate.

"This is the first step toward the long journey I have decided to begin. Many of you might not be knowing me well. But the Asian community and all the minority community knows my name, knows my record, knows my honesty, knows my integrity."

He pauses for effect. It's a speech he spent hours practicing and perfecting.

"I believe in justice. Today because of that, I feel proud that I'm a qualified person to run. Today I pledge here I will not let down any one of you here. I will work for everyone in Middlesex County and the state of New Jersey."

And here, Pradip speaks slower, as if to meet the GOP's message of inclusion halfway: "Not only for my community. . . . This is the first party to give any opportunity to any Asian. We all came with an American Dream. Today you see lots of new faces.

"But I will play as a teammate. I will work with everyone," he concludes.

One by one, members of the GOP, many longtime party faithfuls with silver hair and spectacles, rise to their feet. Suddenly, the Indians in the back are no longer the only ones standing.

9

Downturns

By March, that the U.S. economy is faltering is not even a question. Its effects on visa holders such as Sanku and Lipi are disastrous. For the month of February, the INS reports approving 16,000 filings for H-1B visas. In February of the previous year, that number was exactly double at 32,000.

Lipi stays calm but mentally prepares to receive a pink slip. Contractors like herself will be the first to go, she knows. Some of Lipi's friends were among the 16,000 already laid off at Lucent. They scramble to find other jobs before they have to leave the country.

Such is the predicament of an H-1B visa holder; staying in the United States is entirely hinged to one employer, one job. For those who came in sponsored by so-called body shops, as Lipi did, the onus of finding employment rests with the sponsoring company. After all, in the eyes of the INS, the body shop is the employer. In the meantime, "the bench" grows ever more crowded.

Reports surface of body shops not paying employees on time, or at all.

To be the survivor of the first round of a layoff means more work, Lipi quickly discovers. She starts arriving home at 10:00 P.M., too exhausted to converse about how inefficiently managed she thinks her group is. *I have work, I should be grateful,* she tells herself.

In mid-March, the Dow Jones Industrial Average falls the most number of points in its history. The little the Sarmas sank in Lucent stock last October when it was trading at $30 a share now trades at less than $7.

"If Lucent lays me off, my company has to help me find another job," Lipi says. And since Sanku's job looks more secure, the worst-case scenario would have Lipi switching her visa status to that of dependent. Indeed, the idea of sitting home dependent on anybody is among the worst things Lipi can imagine.

Although she can't fathom being home full time, Lipi is a devoted mother. She and Sanku spend evenings and weekends doting on Chiku. On St. Patrick's Day 2001, he becomes very sick and naps away an afternoon he'd usually be out playing. Lipi interrupts his sleep only to place a cool hand across his feverish forehead. They take his temperature often; 102 is the highest it gets. They take turns sleeping by his side, Lipi and Sanku, concerned but grateful they are home to provide this care. When Chiku gets sick on weekdays, his father can telecommute, but that option is impossible for Lipi, who is needed at the computer at her desk and the one below it, used to test the programs she writes.

On weekends, too, via e-mail and phone calls from India, come the reminders of why they left. Corruption in India, their parents report, is worse than ever. It continues to seep into day-to-day living starting at the upper echelons of government. In March, what becomes known as the Tehelka scandal rocks India and her expatriates across the world. An Internet news site,

Tehelka.com, secretly videotapes footage of senior Indian politicians, bureaucrats, and army officers taking money in connection with a fake defense deal. The scandal forces the president of the ruling party to resign.

Yet to the average Indian citizen, corruption rears its head in other forms. One day, Sanku's brother calls him to report on the status of his audition for All-India Radio. Sanku listens eagerly because he was called back a month after his own audition in Bombay and became a regular contributing singer. In Guwahati, though, Sanku's brother auditions only to be told that the station is still reviewing 1997 applications. *But*, he's told, if he can come up with some money, his 2001 audition can be moved into the tapes of 1997 and treated as being as old as those. Sanku's brother obliges, cognizant of the way his audition has suddenly been tainted. He gives the station manager 100 rupees and a bottle of wine. He never hears back from them.

So, as the Sarmas reach the second anniversary of their arrival, they remain grateful to be in America. Yet it is clear the tide has turned in their new home. A limousine ride and a free hotel stay had greeted them when they came to the United States. Now, high-tech workers are being sent back to India. "We saw things no one else did," Sanku says. "Unprecedented growth, they say."

"We thought this was the way America was when we got here," Lipi adds. "Now I don't know how I have survived in my job this long."

Anti-immigrant sentiment deepens, as it tends to during soft economic times. On websites and in chat rooms debating the United States' border policies, sentiments such as the following are commonplace:

> Why are any special considerations being given to these people?
>
> What about considering us American workers first? . . .

> Y2K is over and there is no longer a crisis or any shortage of American high tech workers. The problem is with Corporate America and their short-sighted views and of course their greed. We American high tech workers are not being trained and as we get older, it gets worse for us. Have you ever wondered why the contract workers in this field are older? We worked all of our lives and supported this country at all levels through taxes and purchases of goods and services. . . . How about doing things for Americans? Don't we deserve your support before foreigners?
>
> Send the H-1B people home like they should if they are not working. Let them come back like any other foreigners have too [sic] for work, etc. Give us American high tech workers back our jobs.

In late March, the INS reports that the number of H-1B petitions has dropped by 30 percent compared to the year before. In fiscal year 2000, companies exhausted the nationwide quota of 115,000 visas in the first six months of the year. But between October 2000 and the beginning of March, they approve petitions on behalf of just 72,000 workers.

It's easy to see why. The top sponsors of the visas used to be companies like Motorola, Cisco, and Intel. These same companies now make headlines every day for plummeting stock prices and massive, widespread layoffs. Lucent, Lipi's employer, ends its first quarter with a $3.7 billion loss.

In India, too, daily headlines track the health of U.S. companies. Software engineers quickly learn who Federal Reserve Chairman Alan Greenspan is and tune in to CNBC or CNN International to learn of the latest rate cuts. Among both H-1B visa holders in the United States and software programmers who dream of emigrating from India, the e-mail messages swarm. They include report after report of Indian programmers, people just like Sanku and Lipi, going home en masse. Yet Lipi looks around and sees no such thing happening. "Everyone's tense but they're not leaving," she says.

An unsigned e-mail circulates on listservs containing an admonishment for those still in India. "People coming on H-1 from very good companies go through a lot of agony and frustration. Hot skills like Java are cold skills now. . . . So please friends don't take the risk of leaving your current job for the sake of a US offer. . . . Wait until the situation improves. This is not to frighten or discourage someone from coming here, use it only as information."

In May, Lipi calls Ashwin, her former supervisor at AT&T. He knows right away why she's calling. "Come to me when you've really lost your job," he says. "I don't want to pull any strings and then have you turn us down."

So for now, all Lipi can do is wait to be laid off. She likes to think it's not coming, but common sense prevails.

In the hallways of Lucent, signs go up asking employees to keep their spirits high. "Don't give up!" the fliers say. "Better days are coming!!!" On the corner of one of the photocopies, someone scribbles, "When?"

Besides worrying over their job security, Lipi and Sanku busy themselves getting ready for Lipi's parents' visit that summer. They live alone in Nazira, a city in northern Assam, but Lipi has been urging them to move farther south to Guwahati, the state's largest city, so her father has better access to health care. She also feels that they need to be closer to their relatives so someone can keep an eye on them. Lipi's brother has been studying at Penn State for almost a year now. In his absence, taking care of the parents falls on their elder sister, Kaberi, a doctor, who lives in Guwahati.

It's not that they can't take care of themselves. Girish Chandra Phukan, sixty-three, and his wife, Kiran, fifty-six, are quite capable. Lipi jokes, though, that sometimes they still seem stuck in another century, left behind by the tech boom that has even pervaded India. Once, her parents tried to send her an e-mail from an Internet café near them. It arrived one month later. "My friends from Hyderabad and Madras can chat with their parents on-line," she laments. "My parents are so low-tech."

On June 9, they arrive, taking over Chiku's bedroom and playing the role of his babysitter while Lipi and Sanku are at work, knowing he is in hands as loving as theirs. Lipi had originally planned to take vacation days to show her parents around, but with her future at Lucent suddenly uncertain, she is scared to take any time off.

So her parents become like so many of India's elderly who find themselves trapped in Middlesex County, deprived of the freedom to buy paan or cold drinks from a vendor down the block. "It's almost like we are handicapped here," says Lipi's father. "Unless they take us, we cannot go anywhere."

To their credit, Sanku and Lipi plan weekend excursions and day trips. They go to Niagara Falls and Lake George. There's a weekend trip to Titusville, a town in northwestern Pennsylvania that her father insists they visit as the birthplace of the oil industry. As they browse the Drake Well Museum, where in 1859 Edwin L. Drake drilled the oil well that launched the modern petroleum industry, Lipi's father marvels at how well preserved everything is. "It's just not like this in India," he says later. "We have so much more history than the United States, but it's not maintained."

In between are dinner parties at the homes of their Assamese family friends. Everyone, it seems, wants to invite her parents over—just as they did in the days she and Sanku first arrived. In July, they spend several days in New York City, taking in the wax museum, the science museum, and other sights. During one of those trips, Lipi's parents make their way to the top of the World Trade Center.

10

Under a Mango Tree

Leafing through the classified section of the *Star-Ledger,* New Jersey's largest newspaper, Harish sighs. "Accounting, clerical, I don't care. I just want to start somewhere. There's lots of advertisements. But there's lots of competition, too."

Last year, Harish finished a series of computer courses in spreadsheets and databases. *Surely that made me a more marketable candidate,* he thinks.

But no one ever calls.

In December, he had said he would wait till January. In January, he says maybe March. In the meantime, he picks up a part-time job at Kohl's, another discount store, in its warehouse division. He hates it; it's more demeaning than the Bradlees job because he has to perform physical labor. He moves inventory for a living now, hoists it onto trucks, takes it off trucks. And one day his shift can begin at 2:00 P.M. and end at 11:00 P.M., while the next day it can start at 8:00 A.M. It makes planning for interviews—not to mention sleep—quite difficult; nonetheless, he continues to wait and look for a better job.

In the days Harish spends waiting, he takes care of his wife and shuttles her to and from the doctor. Kapila, without a license, is made even further immobile with her injury. The doctor tells her she needs to perform physical therapy three times a week for her arm, and Harish decides to quit his job at Kohl's.

Ever the optimist, Kajal tells him he will find something soon. She helps him with his résumé, teaching him how to use job-search sites like Monster.com. She tries to get more hours at ShopRite to bring more money in. Last semester, she ended the semester at Middlesex County College on the dean's list with two A's and two B's. It isn't easy juggling it all, but Kajal doesn't complain.

Every night, the phone rings in the Patel house. Once Caller ID tells them who it is, the household's trio clamors to be the voice to greet Zankhana.

After Zankhana married, she and Bittu tried to make a new life for themselves in New Jersey and to forget the pain their union had caused. For the months after she married, Zankhana became the unspoken word in the Patel house. Kapila cried, and everyone knew why, but it just wasn't talked about.

In the summer of 1996, Zankhana tearfully called her family. "Can you meet me at Shree Ram Mandir?"

Harish and Kapila went and met Zankhana and her husband at their familiar place of worship, a church converted into a Hindu temple in a residential neighborhood. The family went inside together during aarti, the offering to the deities on display throughout the temple. They sat without speaking, praying in silence to the deities surrounding them. As aarti concluded, Harish invited his daughter and son-in-law back to the Hilltop apartment, where Kapila cooked them dinner. It wasn't exactly like old times with Zankhana living at home, but it was a start.

So their reconciliation began, tiptoeing toward each other, then intertwined once again. Still, making new memories in a place filled with such bitter ones proved too hard. Zankhana's husband also found the taxi business far too competitive near New York City and its metropolitan areas. In 1997, he and Zankhana decided to move to Rochester, in upstate New York, to be closer to his cousins. With most of his business coming from the Rochester airport, Bittu only had to do four or five jobs a day to earn what he had been making in New York.

Despite being so far from her own friends and family, Zankhana welcomed the move upstate. She feared living too close to her father. Each day, though, she sees her father in her husband. "My husband is proud, too. That's the problem," she says. "Two proud men can't live in one house."

Harish eventually grew to understand his daughter was really in love, reciprocated by her husband. But why didn't she complete her associate's degree? "I'm very upset that she didn't finish," he still says. "She's very intelligent. The problem now is the baby." Quite visibly, however, Simran is what brought the families even closer, forcing Harish and Kapila and Kajal to venture up to Rochester more regularly—if only to inject Simran's mixed English-Hindi-Punjabi vocabulary with a few words of Gujarati.

Bittu is not as frequent a visitor to the Patel home, begging off the reunions because working weekends and nights means more money. Zankhana knows he must work, but there's more that keeps him away: the implicit judgment Harish passes on his son-in-law every time he sees him, that he is not good enough.

Zankhana doesn't wait for him to say it before she answers his thoughts in everyday conversation. She talks about how busy they are, especially with the baby, how much he provides for her and Simran, how soon they can buy a house. Then she turns to the issue of her husband's lack of education: Maybe he'll go back and get his GED. "But if he studies, how can he provide us food? Whatever he thinks is the best, what can I say."

What *can* she say? Inwardly, she knows her life with Bittu is not perfect. She has sacrificed much for him, and how they will raise Simran—within the polytheistic beliefs of Hinduism or monotheism of Sikhism—remains unclear. "I don't believe in five gods, so we're teaching her there's one god," Zankhana says. On the other hand, Simran has already had her hair cut, as has her father; orthodox followers of Sikhism do not cut their hair out of respect for it as a creation of God and as a sign of their devotion. The same Zankhana who refused to touch meat in the Burger King now cooks chicken curry for her husband and daughter. All she asks is that he buy it boneless. She shudders to think how her family's food once had legs to walk on, wings to flap. Better if someone else removes the bones before she has to handle it.

When Zankhana comes home, she is a married woman with her child, a guest in her former home, according to the cultural mores of India. Many Indian American youth adopt American attitudes toward visits to the in-laws, alternating holidays, treating a wife's home the same as her husband's. But Zankhana can't help but feel that perhaps she *is* a guest. Gone are the days when Harish asked her to make calls on his behalf to prospective employers or his credit card company. Gone are the days when a teenage Zankhana pitched in for the family's groceries and expenses; Harish won't accept her money now.

He instead pins his hopes on Kajal, who has none of Zankhana's temper but also none of her street smarts. Kajal is sweet, innocent. Her family's economic condition forced her to grow up quickly, but she has also lived a sheltered existence. She blow-dries her long black hair straight and sleek; her timid face and occasionally acned cheeks reveal her youth. Kajal loves to move to Bollywood music and takes part in group dances for various cultural functions. Recently, there was a show at Chutney Mary, a catering hall in nearby South Brunswick, and Kajal performed to a packed house. Her father went but her mother did not; tickets cost $20 per person.

Despite her grace, Kajal is not always able to articulate what she wants at work, at school, or for her future. Harish often scolds her for belaboring a point, for dragging stories on, for obsessing over pointless details. Kajal says she just gets nervous. The ShopRite where she works was once a drive-in movie theater, where suburban teenagers sought privacy and freedom. Today, one of the area's busiest supermarkets sits on the site, employing dozens of desi teenagers like Kajal whose hourly wages help support their families.

Kajal has no bank account of her own; she hands her paycheck of about $100 or $150 in a good week to her father. She expects him to return a $20 bill for spending money that week, as he inevitably does. She cares so much what her father thinks, jumping when he raises his voice the slightest bit. She has told him that her family comes first and that when she turns twenty-four she will go with him and Kapila to India to marry a boy of their choosing. Of course, she wants to approve the match, but she expects them to set up the initial meeting.

Such an attitude is uncommon for women like Kajal raised in the United States. Their male counterparts are more likely the ones who will return to India and find a bride, and even that seems rare. Rather, the matrimonial fate of desi youth in the United States has become an industry in and of itself, domestic in every sense of the word. On American-based websites like A-1M.com or MerePyar.com, which boast hundreds of advertisements, parents or prospects themselves fill out an online form with their preferred age range, religion, caste, region, and profession. For those who don't trust the Internet, desi singles nights are organized by various networking and professional organizations. Speed dating, too, has become a common practice, where men and women rotate talking to one another for seven minutes. At the end of an hour or two, they each enumerate the promising candidates they wouldn't mind talking to again—hoping the others feel the same way. More recently have come actual matrimonial conventions, staged annually, where youth from certain parts of India are thrust together in the hopes they will hit it off. And then there are always personal ads, a method already familiar to many Americans. Yet the ads in ethnic newspapers like *India Abroad* or *News India-Times* contain a specificity rarely seen in their mainstream counterparts:

> ALLIANCE invited for very fair Hindu boy 29/5'11"/160 pounds. B. Tech software engineer, USA. Email: weddingbells29@. . . .

Saying "fair," those who invite the alliance are talking not about the young man's just nature but his skin tone. Most ads make reference to one's size and coloring; if they don't, readers assume the marriage seeker is dark and fat.

Ads tend to be caste specific. It's not enough to be a Jain; one must be Swetambar Jain Marwari. Sikhs specify if they want JatSikhs, while Gujaratis spell out the last name they are looking to unite with, such as Patel or Vaishnav.

> PARENTS seek professional JatSikh boy for 24/5'7" daughter completing law school. Slim, fair, athletic, cultured, US born, speaks Punjabi fluently, holds strong family values.

Even "flaws" can be explained away in these advertisements. Take divorce, a growing phenomenon in India yet among its diaspora still a cultural taboo:

> 37/5'7 1/2" look much younger, good looking Hindu Gujarati professional. *Issueless* innocent divorcee. Working as Sr. Software Consultant, MS Computer Science. Easy going, down to earth, cosmopolitan outlook, good sense of humor. Seeking attractive girl. Caste, religion absolutely no bar. . . .

Such contrived methods of meeting are rarely the stuff of Bollywood movies, the kind Kajal watches with her parents on so many nights that transport her far, far from the couch she sleeps on, the cash register she punches, the computer books she reads. Harish, Kajal, and Kapila often spend their nights watching Hindi movies and serials—Indian soap operas—rented for a dollar per tape. At such a cheap price, there's no question they are pirated, mass-produced for audiences either too eager or too thrifty to watch them on the big screen in nearby second-run theaters that have converted to Indian movie houses to survive.

When asked what he really wishes he could do for a living, Harish thinks for a long time. Perhaps it's because he's so rarely asked, or maybe those thoughts don't even dare be wished anymore.

"I want to own a video store . . . like for Bollywood movies and serials."

Bollywood, India's vast film industry—the name is a play on the obvious—is estimated to churn out more movies than any other country. Almost all the productions are musicals, and often a movie's success depends on the quality of its songs and dances. Story lines are simple: boy meets girl, loses girl, and fights all obstacles to gain her back. In India, predictability has led to popularity. Bollywood rakes in close to $8 billion a year, with more than a quarter of that grossed in the United States.

For immigrants, the attachment to Bollywood is understandably a connection to their past. For young people like Payal and Toral, it's a connection to a culture they have never really lived. But for viewers in India, it's an escape from the everyday. Two people are brought together, torn apart, then reunited. Movies with tragic endings fare less well in India than those that follow the tried-and-true formula. Some say the theme of unification reflects directly on the bloody divorce India and Pakistan underwent in the Partition of 1947; metaphorically speaking, moviegoers represent the wronged children who hope their parents will get back together. What's certain is that Bollywood offers an escape from the ordinary, a glimmer that perhaps everything can turn out happily ever after. This is what makes Harish's dream job so poignant.

What Harish remembers of Baroda and what is true blur somewhere in the nostalgia that defines the memories of so many immigrants like him. It's been years since the Patels have been to India. Each year, they plan to go, but a scarcity of money always forces them to abandon the trip. Still, they feel the need to fill the wish lists of their nieces and nephews however possible, so when they hear of people going to India, they ask them to cart the items over. "He doesn't just want sneakers," Harish says of his nephew. "They have to be Nikes or Reeboks."

In Baroda, though, their friends and family reciprocate the favor, sending salwar kameezes and jewelry for the women and tailored shirts for Harish. Among the most frequent presenters of gifts are Kemas Wadia, the son of Harish's old friend and neighbor, and his wife, Kurshid. In April 2001, as they drive through the crowded streets of Baroda, Kemas passes dozens of stalls with brightly colored salwar kameezes hanging from the shops' entryways. "Zankhana would like one of those," Kemas says in Gujarati.

The ties to Baroda also remain strong for Kajal, even though she was just a little girl when she left. She faithfully writes letters to Amit Vaidya, her former schoolteacher, who offered tuition, or tutoring, after school. "Kajal was very disciplined," Amit recalls. "She used to spend the whole day with me sometimes, at school and then tuition. Her father wasn't here a lot because he was in America. So I like to think I was like her father."

Amit, whose family lives in a nearby farming village, has taken to corresponding with Kajal more by e-mail. He knows many Gujaratis in New Jersey and prides himself on keeping up with American pop culture. For example, he wears a baseball cap emblazoned with the words "L.A. Lakers."

While American sports teams have made fans out of Baroda's residents, some parts of Baroda remain as Harish left them. The Bank of Baroda, for example, looks much as Harish describes. The main room still requires patrons to stand on separate lines for each function from cash receipts to cash payments. The lines are as long as he promised they would be. And it's still not air-conditioned.

Many of the bank's employees remember Harish. R. C. Patel, a man who looks about Harish's age, says they worked together. "Harish was very happy here, but he wanted more because of his family. This is the situation of the Indian people."

Patel is a deputy general manager for the bank, a rank it took him thirty-five years to attain. "I am very happy here. Here is a very secure job, very secure life. You cannot lose your job in a bank," he says. "But so many people have left the bank and gone to America. . . . They want to migrate to the U.S.A. for the future of their kids. So many of them are in New Jersey. They stay in New Jersey because their whole families are there." He recalls Harish as a middle manager and says money was always tight.

Later, back in the car rumbling over Baroda's bumpy roads, Kemas echoes that sentiment. "He had a very hard life here. He struggled to pay off debts."

He falls silent as he nears Harish and Kapila's home, which they still own. Kemas checks in on it every now and then as a favor. The house sits off a main paved road on a dirt one, wide enough for just one car.

The dream house Harish speaks of is the only one on the block with just one floor. The renters, a family of three, come to the door to greet Kemas, who is carrying his son Danish. The hosts graciously offer tea and biscuits and say little.

A tour of the home doesn't last long. The family lives out of the room one enters, which serves as living room, bedroom, and dining room. They pay 700 rupees—less than $20 these days—to Kapila's nephew every month and are hoping to buy their own place soon. Their daughter plays on a mat on the floor; her head is shaven, after a Hindu ritual commemorating her third birthday. A door to her left remains padlocked. Kemas explains: inside that room are the possessions the Patels left behind in July 1990.

Before leaving, Kemas takes his son out back and up the concrete stairs to the roof. He points out the thick branches of the mango tree nearby. "Harish used to come home from work and eat mangoes here," he says. The tree's branches shade both the roof and a field, one of the few, it seems, in otherwise congested Baroda. A walk across the roof yields a view of the dirt road where one man peddles eggs and another a bicycle. The flatness of the roof will allow Harish to build more stories if he ever returns. Reality meets Harish's nostalgia; this is a most peaceful place.

11

Meeting Elephants

Pradip "Peter" Kothari's name lines Oak Tree Road, sandwiched between two elephants that stand for the GOP. His name graces fliers on a few telephone poles, a sign on his front lawn, and the bumpers of his family's cars. It's almost as if the mark he made on the community over the last decade is official now.

Never one to shun attention, Pradip rises to the occasion, surrounded by a trusty entourage of young men who advise him on what to say, what to write, what to wear. On June 4, 2001, he sends a form letter to all the reporters who have been calling him for years: "My candidacy for Freeholder of Middlesex County, NJ, as a Republican is indeed a very bold and historic step for both our community and myself. My victory will write a glorious chapter in the annals of the rapidly growing talented and resourceful Indian American Leaders. With the pen and the power of the pen behind you, I feel it will contribute immensely in educating the voters and mobilizing support for myself."

Four days later, Pradip holds a fund-raiser unlike any a freeholder candidate in Middlesex County has held before. First, there's its size. About a thousand people, mostly Indians but a handful of others as well, pack the ballroom of Royal Albert's Palace. The program for the evening depicts Pradip's face against the red, white, and blue of the American flag. The names of the invited special guests on the cover are preceded by "Hon."; they are members of the political community Pradip wishes to penetrate. The most influential is Bob Franks, who ran for the U.S. Senate the year Pradip didn't vote for him and is now challenging Jersey City mayor Bret Schundler for the GOP gubernatorial bid. But the names on the list inside of the program, designated the host committee, look more like the faces in the crowd. There are the usual Pradip supporters, of course, such as restaurant owners Chandrakant Patel of Chowpatty and Jaswant Singh of Ashoka. But there's also a range of professions listed beside the names from mechanic to otolaryngologist, of businesses owned from Iselin Pharmacy to Jai Jalaram Sweet House. The minority of white people in the room stick together, as do the brown. One man says to his wife: "I can't eat spicy food. I hope I do okay here." The songs of Daler Mehndi, a renowned turbaned Punjabi singer, blasts from speakers. As the bhangra beats throughout the room, attendees tap their feet while they wait for the program to start.

Out front, Payal and Toral and employees from the travel agency wrangle the hordes and ensure all have paid the $150 per couple to enter. "How many Patels *are* there in the world?" Toral whispers to Payal. It's chaotic, and some people don't want to pay or insist they already have. Toral, tired of arguing, just lets them in.

Inside, bunches of red, white, and blue balloons dot the ballroom, and an American flag and an Indian flag crisscross above the makeshift stage. The balloons are anchored to the tables by ceramic elephants, an ironic meeting of the GOP symbol and Indian art. The banner laid out reads, "Welcome to a star-spangled reception"; the salutation is printed between Indian and American flags. When the program begins and the VIPs are introduced, bhangra music blasts as they walk on. It's almost a repeat of the night Pradip was named a candidate, with friend after friend praising his leadership ability and virtue. But unlike at the GOP convention, this crowd is almost entirely Indian and almost entirely composed of new entrants to the political scene.

"In India, they say children are born politicians," says H. R. Shah, the owner of TV Asia.

Another supporter follows with, "There's politics in his blood."

Among the handful of non-Indians who speak is Reggie Johnson, chairman of the NAACP in Metuchen. He recalls the day when TKR, a cable company, announced it was dropping the BET, a television network serving African Americans. Pradip called him right away, Johnson recounts. "They're dropping TV Asia, too," Pradip told him. "You get your people and I'll get mine. Let's protest at TKR on Friday."

Turning to Pradip, Johnson says "his people" will once again be there for him.

As they speak, Pradip sits next to his wife at a front table. He occasionally claps for himself.

"Every time a glass breaks, Peter becomes stronger and stronger," says Mahesh Shah, owner of a string of car-repair shops, referring to the smashed windows that stirred Pradip to action in the first place.

Finally, as Pradip is called to the microphone, the audience joins him in rising. He carries no speech and starts to address the crowd, quieting the standing ovation. "For twelve years, I did a great job for our community. I always wanted to lead my community to destiny. So many people can disagree with me and join together for a common cause." He swallows. "But our community *must* have a voice in government."

When the applause subsides, Pradip takes up the matter of Woodbridge mayor Jim McGreevey, his onetime ally and Bob Franks's opponent,. He addresses him as if he were there, although this is the last place he'd be on a night like this. "For twelve years, you did nothing. No more promises."

He concludes with the words "Long live America," then tacks on two more phrases absent at his last political speech before the Republicans: "Long live India. Jai Hind."

Red, white, and blue confetti scatters through the air like snowflakes. Some lands in Pradip's hair as he raises his hands to wave at the crowd.

His campaign manager, Jesal Amin, introduces Bob Franks, who addresses the crowd with the "Namaste" they are used to; his awkward pronunciation is forgiven. Franks keeps his remarks short, vowing that "if Indian Americans have problems, Peter Kothari will get on the phone with the governor. There are minority communities banging on the door desperate to be a full partner."

Even as he speaks, people in the back approach the buffet tables and start to help themselves. Soon, most of the room is abuzz in conversation, ignoring what's going on up front, where Pradip and his supporters stand. By the time the speeches and thank-yous end, much of the room has finished dinner.

Even Toral and Payal abandon their posts out front and come in to eat. They are used to the spotlight on their father, and tonight is just one more event in a sea of events they have attended to support him.

Toral has recently been focused on a upcoming major event of her own—graduation. She's decided to attend New York University in the fall. After weeks of procrastinating the actual writing of her salutatorian's speech, Toral quickly types some words out before the rehearsal. And that's precisely what she tells the crowd gathered on the Colonia High School football field to see her and 380 others graduate.

"What could I possibly say that would reach each one of you in the sea of distinct and unique faces that form the Class of 2001, who sit before me today? The obvious answer to this complex task was procrastination, something I'm sure each and every one of us has been exposed to at one or several points during these past four years at Colonia. So, at one o'clock on a Wednesday afternoon, I turned NBC on, engrossed in the twisted plot of *Days of Our Lives*. After which, I ate, ran errands, went online, slept, ate again . . . did almost anything imaginable to stray away from the inevitable. By the end of the night, my accomplishment consisted of one word on an enormously blank piece of paper."

She waits for the crowd's laughter to trail off before plunging forward. "Picture waking up at five in the morning, dressing yourself in dirty, torn clothes, working in the fields all day, and coming home to your sick mother, who has developed pneumonia, which could easily have been treated if you were financially and technologically capable. This is life in a Third World society."

Pradip, who is supposed to leave the graduation early for a meeting, perks up. Perhaps his daughter has been listening to him all these years after all?

Toral then jokes that her peers know hardship, too. She enumerates: "Waking up at seven in the morning, what we perceive to be the crack of dawn, driving to school in a Civic instead of the Beamer we dream of, walking in the sticky hallways, wishing our school provided us with central air-conditioning, and complaining about the cafeteria food because we can't leave to grab some Mickey D's."

The rest of Toral's speech reminds the suburban teenagers how lucky they are to be where they are. She winds down not with the prophetic words of Gandhi or Martin Luther King but with

> You're on your own. And you know what you know.
> And YOU are the one who'll decide where to go. . . .
> Wherever you fly, you'll be best of the best.
> Wherever you go, you will top all the rest.

"Dr. Seuss," Toral pronounces to applause.

After she receives her diploma, moves her tassel, and throws her cap into the air, Toral goes to find her family. "Dad," she says, seeing Pradip, "you stayed?"

"You should be writing my speeches," he tells her with a hug.

They might not write his speeches, but Payal and Toral are trying to help their dad all they can. "We're all for it," says Payal.

On the day of the primary, Payal and Nandini station themselves at Quick Travel's offices to remind people to go out and vote. It is a right they cannot exercise today, as both are still registered as Democrats.

Pradip spends the day at Middlesex County's Republican headquarters, a building that resembles an insurance office on Victorian Plaza, a strip mall. And there, on a day he thinks voting is just a formality, Pradip finds out he has lost.

Not only does he lose, he loses to people who didn't even want to win. Audrey Cornish and Arthur Hasselback tell newspapers that they only agreed to appear on the ballot to round out former Jersey City mayor Bret Schundler's candidacy. Schundler defeats Bob Franks in the Republican primary, and Cornish and Hasselback ride his coattails for the win. This scenario isn't unheard of in the local politics of a closed primary. In a Republican primary, of course, only registered Republicans can vote, so voters tend to be more conservative—enabling them, in this case, to defeat Franks, who was the party favorite and the more moderate of the two candidates.

The loss is stinging. Pradip had been the only one to hold a fund-raiser, a lavish one that made the party's usual spaghetti dinners and meetings at the Elks Lodge look downright parochial. They had *asked* him to run, after all. He had been touted as the future of the party.

As the state GOP—now under Schundler's leadership—tries to figure out what to do with its reluctant county candidates, Pradip wonders where that leaves him. One possibility, he's been told, is that the party brass can put him back on the ballot. But if he couldn't win in the primary, what will be his fate in the general election in a county that is so heavily Democratic?

"I was caught off guard," he says a week after the failed primary. "For the Republican Party, I am still new. For so long, I was unaffiliated with them. And we never energized them. . . . I just didn't think we had a primary. I hear they might try to convince me to run, but I don't want to base any decision on hearsay."

Yet even as he speaks, the "Vote for Peter" signs remain hanging in the windows of his travel agency; the bumper stickers are still affixed to his Dodge Caravan parked out back.

It turns out there's no need to take them down. By summer's end, it's official. Pradip Kothari and Tina Martins Cruz, a South River lawyer who is the daughter of Portuguese immigrants, are back on the ballot, along with Tracy Ford, a patient-equipment technician with four children. Ford, a black New Brunswick activist, was the only one of the three candidates who had won the primary. Reacting to the new slate, Schundler says, "We want to be the party that serves the people, and we want our party to look like the people."

Once Pradip is reinstated in the race, his life again becomes defined by the local campaign trail. There are parades to wave in, photos to be taken for brochures, community groups and block associations to meet with. Unlike the other candidates', Pradip's campaign seems to extend far beyond Middlesex County's, even New Jersey's, borders. He garners national attention from the ethnic press; the image of him with his arms raised graces front covers and inside pages as though, somehow, he's already been victorious. By running in the election of 2001, Pradip joins a handful of Indian American candidates across the country. In an article about the phenomenon, one writer reports, "The list of Indian candidates is growing and their campaigns are gaining momentum, forcing their voices to be heard—a privilege which was once denied to immigrants." Unlike Pradip, most are running on the Democratic ticket. Renu Lobo, a broadcast journalist, Inderjit Singh, a Sikh man, and Jairam Thakral, a Pakistani-born man raised in Indian Punjab after Partition, all seek seats on the New York City Council—a body that has never seen a single Asian American elected. And in New Jersey, Franklin Township mayor Upendra Chivukula—who has already achieved one victory—aspires to be the state's first Indian American legislator. Telling a reporter how it felt to win once, the mayor says, "It was a terrific moment when all these white Americans lifted me off the ground and congratulated me. I will never forget it."

On August 15, India's Independence Day, Pradip dons a white suit and marches in the annual India Day Parade down Madison Avenue. Few of the spectators live in Middlesex County. Still, he knows that enough Indians with connections to New Jersey will be attending to make it worth his while. Besides, this is the very parade that launched his return to public work. Payal and Toral walk behind him, dressed in Indian outfits like most of the parade's participants; Nandini is at work. Hours later, Payal and Toral change into their club gear to dance the night away at Cheetah, where the parade's afterparty is being held.

On August 26, Toral begins life as a New Yorker, no longer able to be classified as a part of the "bridge and tunnel" crowd she and Payal represented that night at Cheetah. As she begins her freshman year at New York University, in its prestigious business scholars program, Toral grapples with pangs of loneliness, missing her old friends and her family. "I miss my Mom and Dad," she says less than a week into the semester. "Everybody's really dorky here."

Calls from Nandini are frequent. "You are there to study, you know."

Toral, as Nandini is well aware, has already tapped into NYU's vibrant desi scene. "It's really weird at NYU, but everyone knows someone who knows someone," Toral says. One of her best friends is a sophomore, the daughter of another Indian community leader in New Jersey. "My roommates are all white," Toral says, adding, "but they are really cool."

Indeed, the Kothari girls have been raised with the ability to weave in and out of cultures. In his campaign, Pradip's own ability to do so is put to the test. This is certainly true at the annual Labor Day Parade in South Plainfield, an emblem of suburban-bred patriotism with its stream of veterans marching. Spectators include children straining to catch a glimpse of a fire truck, teenagers who want to show off their new clothes and tans before school starts, and parents cheering on their football players, cheerleaders, and Scouts.

Few faces look like Pradip's as he joins the Republican Party contingent assembling on a side street. He rides with Tina Martins Cruz in the back of her husband's pickup truck, atop bales of hay. Tracy Ford is clearly the odd man out, having just met the other two; he has seated his massive frame on the other side of the truck. Tina asks Pradip what their platform might be. Because they were just put back on the ballot, they have no campaign literature showing all three of them.

The truck passes a house of twenty- and thirtysomethings out barbecuing, and they ask the trio to get down and say a few words. Pradip obliges, then hops back onto his bale of hay to resume the parade route. The spectators continue to cheer and wave the flags that are brought out just a few patriotic times a year.

It is just days before September 11. Soon the flags will fly again.

12

Farewells

Lipi survives Lucent's round of layoffs in July, but not those in August. She is among the last ten people of her group asked to leave. The first phone call she makes is to Ashwin, her old boss at AT&T, who not only pushes his bosses to rehire her but schedules her start date for late September so she can finally spend time with her parents, who are still in the States.

That's what she's doing on September 11. They are sitting on the couch watching television when suddenly there is just one image on all the networks: towers burning, then falling. People running, people crying. Sanku calls from work; he's on his way home and will pick up Chiku from day care. The family remains glued to the television for the rest of the day, not even bothering to monitor it as they usually do for Chiku's young eyes.

When he sits down some days later to write how he feels, Lipi's father, Girish Chandra Phukan, thinks of the view from the World Trade Center's observation deck not so long ago. It had been a clear July day when they ventured into New York City. He had seen the towers from miles away, when he was still in New Jersey, and recognized them immediately as the stock image of New York City, of America even, he'd seen for decades. When he finally made it to the top at age sixty-four, he'd felt as if he were on the top of the world gazing downward at the ants of civilization; to the west was a running river, the one he had just crossed to get here.

"Tears of the Hudson," he titles the work in Assamese. Starting with a lake in the Adirondack Mountains, he describes how the world's bodies of water suddenly became receptacles for the river's tears.

Two columns were created on your bank
In a life full of struggle
You nursed them both with tender care
Earning fame in the world with a high head
They sang your praises and glory standing from the bank
In a heartless assault
Your twin towers were violated
And stunning the whole world, they fell down
In your sweet lap.

Like everyone else, central New Jersey's Indians mourn the loss of neighbors and friends, the loss of their skyline and compass, in the attacks of September 11. But those in brown skin have conflicting emotions on what's happened. America is supposed to be an escape. All these years, the calls in the middle of the night have been over riots, assassinations, or earthquakes over there, not here. Now their relatives scramble to get hold of them to see if they are safe. In America?

For Sanku the attacks hark back to the only wartime he ever knew: the agitation in Assam of the 1980s. Every night, he went to bed with his socks still on because he had to be prepared to run.

Assam's years of strife reflected a medley of conflicts whose sources included an influx of refugees from neighboring Bangladesh and Nepal as well as an Indian government that neglected Assam's infrastructure. Throughout the 1970s and 1980s, movements sprang up to outlaw all languages but Assamese, to deport all illegal immigrants and refugees, and, perhaps most drastic, to officially secede from India. For much of Sanku's youth in the 1980s, he remembers, protest rallies and armed militia lining the streets near his home were commonplace. Seeing the National Guard nearly twenty years later in the suburbs of Edison brings back those surreal memories. He remembers the chants of "Tej dim, tel nidieu"—"We'll give you blood, but not our oil"—referring to what many Assamese perceived as an exploitation of their natural resources by the central government. Old ladies and young boys would gather to block access to Assam's refineries; protests in those days felt more like festivals, Sanku recalls now, not as fear-ridden. Or perhaps it had been the exuberance of youth, of believing in a cause, that had made him so fearless.

"Still, this is the safest place," Sanku tells Lipi four Saturday afternoons after the attacks. "Tolerance is not very high in Pakistan or India. If this happened to us, we'd take up guns."

"Siblings fight the hardest," Lipi retorts, referring to India and Pakistan. Both she and Sanku watch the news intently as the United States aligns itself with Pakistan in order to invade Afghanistan. "All the Asian countries are going to erupt now. Brown skin is not going to be trusted," Lipi observes. "But in one month, Americans will forget about the bombs they've dropped."

In New Jersey, there's safety in numbers. Despite reports of a backlash against immigrants, especially those from South Asia and the Middle East, Sanku and Lipi say they experience none of it.

Two people, however, are killed in incidents ruled to be driven by bias, a need to retaliate, a need to blame. Both men killed are South Asian—one Pakistani Muslim in Texas, one Indian Sikh in Arizona. That, too, injects fear into many of New Jersey's Indians. Worried, Lipi and her family call her brother at Penn State.

"Shave off your goatee," she tells him.

"I already did it," comes the response.

September 11 affects the job security of many people, Sanku and Lipi among them. The attacks take an already shaky economy and throw it straight into recession.

When Lipi reports to work in late September, there's a comforting familiarity in working at the company that brought her to the United States. She counts down the days till her green card is processed, waiting for the day when she can be on a par with other Americans. It's been an anxious year for her. Months ago, as President George W. Bush spoke of granting amnesty to undocumented Mexican workers, Lipi had bitterly watched the news and said, "Maybe I should go into landscaping, too."

September 11 changes U.S. immigration policy, as wartime tends to do. Immigration drops nearly 20 percent in the six months after the attacks.

Yet September 11 also strengthens the Americanness of Lipi and Sanku. It strengthens their desire to belong, to complete the dream they began less than three years ago. They start to go house-hunting and compare mortgage rates. They look beyond Edison, for it's getting too crowded for their liking. Like the once city-dwelling Indians who settled in these suburbs, they look farther south.

When Lipi's parents ready themselves to return home to India, the Sarmas are still in the process of looking for the perfect home. A few days before his grandparents are to leave, Chiku cries. "I want you to stay here forever," he says to his grandfather, with his arms around his wrinkled neck.

Seeing this, Lipi's mother chokes up. "Now he understands what it is to have family outside his mother and father. That is what children like him don't have in this country."

After all the times she has said good-bye to her family and stayed stoic, Lipi sheds tears as her parents board the flight. The urge to go with them, to return to India, subsides as Lipi, Sanku, and Chiku drive back from the airport to Edison, to home.

13

The Festival Family

Just before 9:00 A.M. on September 11, Toral is in her room getting ready for Expository Writing when she hears a buzz.

"That plane is awfully close to—"

Toral's roommate never finishes the sentence, and a loud boom fills lower Manhattan. The girls see the smoke and observe people below their West Village window craning their necks upward. Even after the second plane hits several minutes later, Toral continues to ready herself for class.

Class, of course, is canceled, as it remains for the next three days. There are frantic calls from Mom and Dad, but Toral, as scared as she is, stays in the city until the weekend. She buys disposable cameras; the film developer can process the images quicker than she can. She tries to make sense of it along with the other college freshmen, who are urged to attend counseling sessions and floor meetings to discuss their feelings. Some leave the city; others vow to stay. She hears from some Sikh classmates who have been taunted, Indian guys who have been told to go back where they came from.

Back on Oak Tree Road, Pradip works to minimize a backlash in a section of town that faced prejudice long before September 11. As a candidate for office, though, he realizes he must also remain patriotic, must wave the flag, must be more American than anyone else. Luckily, the reaction in the community means he doesn't have to fake it.

"After September 11, there was not even one incident," he says. Prayer meetings with Muslims, Sikhs, and Christians become popular campaign stops for the month of September. For despite the tragedy, the campaign must go on.

So must celebrations, although it's not quite the same. For a few moments, Pradip and his festival committee contemplate canceling this year's Navratri. They fear a tent full of Indians dancing in the aftermath of the attacks sends the wrong message, and with potentially thousands of South Asians showing up, they fear both terrorists and bigots may attack. But Pradip, a newly loyal member of the GOP, decides to follow the advice of the nation's highest-ranking Republican.

"When President Bush appealed to the people to facilitate the return to normalcy and not submit to the terrorists, we decided to go ahead with Navratri," he tells a reporter from *India Abroad*. "We put together the show in just two weeks."

On October 12, once again the dancing begins. Payal is in a dreamlike state as she thinks of a boy she met just two and a half weeks ago. "But," she points out when made fun of, "he's called me every night, so it feels like much longer. He's very romantic." The gushing continues. *He's so smart. He's 23. He, like, made a computer. He's five-foot-nine.* She gestures several inches above her temple. *Well, almost.*

Toral, patient during most of the description, rolls her eyes. "I need a man," she whines. "Let's go dance."

In the last year, Toral has blossomed in every way. She was recently selected as a finalist for *Teen People* magazine's most-beautiful-people feature. Nandini looks at her and can't help but think her daughter's turned into a woman.

Well, most days. On the Friday before Election Day, Toral runs around the house with a Garfield nightie over the bottom of her lehenga. As always, she, Payal, and her mom are running a little late.

"I've been so busy," says Nandini. She's working at four hospitals now and feels she hasn't given Pradip's festival and campaign the attention they deserve. "In the past, I used to always be there with him. Printing tickets, answering phones. I cannot do it like before."

Still, she frets about her husband's fate. While she remains optimistic, she fears his disappointment if he does not win. "If the Indians vote, we will win, I know it," she says. "But a lot of them are jealous. And the others—why vote for someone you don't know?"

Payal stands in front of the bathroom mirror applying makeup to her face and neck, still thinking of her conversation with her latest crush last night. Her mother calls for her.

"What earrings will you wear, Payal?" Nandini hands her a pair, not waiting for the answer.

Payal puts on the earrings. They loop over her ears in a style worn in India hundreds of years ago. It's making a comeback—but not for Payal tonight.

"Mom," she says, "I look like an alien." She takes them off and opts for a smaller pair.

"Payal, I need help with my paloo," says Nandini, fidgeting with the portion of her sari that drapes over her right side.

The phone rings. Payal answers, and her face lights up.

"Payal, I cannot hold this forever. I need help pinning it." Nandini is holding the creases in the pink netting away from her shoulder. She knows her daughter is on the phone with someone suddenly deemed more important than Mom.

Into the phone, Payal says she needs to go. But the banter continues for a few more minutes.

"Payal." Nandini knows it's a boy.

"Can I just call you back?"

As Payal fastens a pin to her mom's blouse, the doorbell rings.

"Who is that? Toral, go get it."

From the bedroom, Payal can hear her sister say, "Oh my gosh, what are *you* doing here?"

Then they hear, "She's upstairs, go ahead."

In walks a young man with a baseball cap, a bright yellow shirt, and jeans hanging well beyond his ankles. Payal screams, not a scary scream but the high-pitched shriek of teenage girls at a slumber party. As the young man notices her mother, he sheepishly goes to sit down in the living room, without saying a word. Payal whispers to her mother.

"Isn't that so sweet, he surprised me. Who does that, Mom?"

"You like him?" Nandini asks.

Payal doesn't answer except to say: "Mom, he's Guju."

Nandini laughs.

"And he's Swaminarayan."

"Like us," says Nandini.

When they arrive at Navratri, the girls take positions in a circle—the same places as last year, only now Payal has company—and begin to dance. At 2:00 A.M., they shake off friends and potential boyfriends to join Pradip and Nandini for aarti. Another year has begun.

14

Classified

It's too late to go back now. Sometimes Harish gets angry and wants to cut his citizenship certificate in two. But on September 11, like so many immigrants who never found the America that was supposed to be, Harish feels a renewed sense of belonging to his adopted country.

It's been a hard summer on his family for sure. As soon as Kapila returns to work, she learns it will be short-lived. Her employer's lease in Raritan Center about to expire, and the company is moving its operations to Virginia. In the meantime, Kapila tries to rack up as much overtime as possible. Harish's job in a furniture warehouse is gone almost as soon as he starts it. He's working now as a security guard on weekends but still seeking full-time work. "I am used to these situations now," he says.

After the attacks, the Patels take great pains to show their Americanness, adorning their home with flags. From ShopRite, Kajal purchases a picture of the World Trade Center as it used to be. "These acts shattered American steel but they cannot dent the steel of American resolve," it reads. They hang it by the door, above the piles of shoes they take off before entering the apartment.

On October 27, a night of Navratri, Kapila, dressed in the top of a salwar kameez and a white petticoat, helps Kajal and her friends get dressed. She's in a good mood today, having worked three and a half hours of overtime this morning. Harish is still at work and won't be home till after midnight. Sonali and Nipa, two girls from Hilltop, are primping in the mirror in Harish, Kapila, and Kajal's room, which is crammed with Bollywood posters, outdated calendars of Hindu gods, and suitcases stacked several feet high. Nipa works with Kajal at ShopRite and also attends Middlesex. She's full of energy tonight, cracking jokes in Gujarati as she weaves the front of Kajal's hair into two thin braids framing her face. She looks older this year than last, her skin suddenly clearer, her posture more confident. As she paces before the full-length mirror, the bells on her payal, or anklets, jangle lightly.

"Do I look like a dork?" she asks.

Sonali and Nipa assure her she looks lovely. Before they leave, the phone rings. It's Zankhana. Bittu's on the overnight shift, and Simran's acting up.

"Let me talk to her." Kapila asks Kajal to hand her the phone.

"She'll be on the phone for hours now." Kajal hands over the phone as she prepares to leave. She hopes Zankhana can make it down for at least one night of Navratri before it ends in November. On the phone just now, Zankhana promised to try.

Nipa has driven her car over, assuring her father that Kajal will take her to Expo Hall. But Kajal, who got into an accident a few months ago, has been forbidden from driving at night. So Nipa takes her car, saying her father will never understand.

The security at Expo seems somewhat tighter this time, perhaps because of September 11, perhaps because this is the actual weekend of Navratri and crowds will be large. As they embrace friends they haven't seen since for a week or more, Nipa is quick to comment on the cute boys all around. As usual, Kajal remains silent on the subject.

On the ride over, though, she'd said she isn't sure if she could allow her parents to so readily choose someone for her after all. "My father wants a doctor or lawyer from India. But I think I might want someone who grew up here like me."

One of the cute boys comes over to talk to Kajal. Her face lights up; she laughs and fiddles with her braids. Then he says, "I need your help hooking me up with that woman over there." Kajal's face is about to fall, but she perks up when Sonali announces she's ready to dance.

Kajal has to work tomorrow morning, but she and Nipa and Sonali dance till 1:00 A.M., perform aarti, and split plates of pau bhaji, dipping the bun into the spicy vegetable curry and licking their fingers. Who they will marry, whether Kajal will get into Rutgers, whether Harish will find another job, and what Kapila will do when her employer moves seem like far-off questions tonight as Kajal spins with her friends and clangs her sticks against theirs.

When she gets home around 4:00 A.M., Kajal removes the payal jangling on her feet, the choker around her neck, and puts on her pajamas. She is quiet, so as not to wake her parents. She crawls onto the couch and goes to sleep.

The next morning, Kapila makes Kajal's breakfast as she rushes to get out of the house five minutes before the 10:00 A.M. shift at ShopRite starts. Even after Kajal leaves, Kapila remains in the kitchen, washing dishes and making tea. Harish awakes shortly after and grabs the classified section off the coffee table.

15

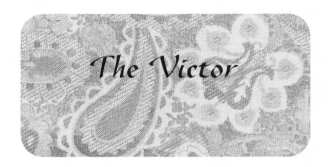

The Victor

On Pradip's first Election Day as a Republican, he displays little of the optimism that has marked his campaign. "Whether it's win or lose," he says after voting around 11:00 A.M., "it was important for us to be in the game."

He spends the day in his campaign headquarters, an office carved out of a home in a residential neighborhood in Iselin. It's filled with volunteers, all desi, all male.

Around 4:00 P.M., a man walks in talking on his cell phone, getting tallies for voter turnout. "Jersey City turnout bahut accha hai," he says in Hindi. Jersey City's turnout is very good.

Some of the volunteers haven't even been able to vote for Pradip—they either live in other counties or aren't yet citizens—but they fill the house, which serves as headquarters for an import-export business, using each phone line and then resorting to the fax machines. Each is given a portion of a list of registered Indian voters.

"Hi, is this Mr. Chopra? I'm calling from Pradip 'Peter' Kothari's office. Just wanted to remind you to go out and vote today. And be sure to vote for Peter Kothari."

Volunteer Himanshu Majmudar places phone call after phone call and inserts an occasional Hindi phrase into his solicitations. He pauses between calls and leans back against the chair. "I used to be in insurance. This is taking me back. Half the time I want to say, 'This is Himanshu from MetLife."

When one Mrs. Parul Patel gets a phone call, she tells the volunteer she has already voted but wants to talk to Pradip himself. Pradip obliges and picks up the line.

"Hello, Mrs. Patel? Thank you for voting today. How long have you been in this country? Oh, fourteen, fifteen years. Long time." He nods and smiles. "You work for the post office? Okay, well, if you're ever on Oak Tree Road, please stop by my office. But make sure you get more involved if you are interested in our community."

With that, he hangs up and turns to the fleet of volunteers. "What the outcome is is not that important really. We are writing a chapter in a book here."

Mahesh Shah, the auto mechanic, sits nearby and nods. "Here's a guy who switched parties knowing fully well that it's hard to win as a Republican in Middlesex County. There was not a single Indian candidate before him. But they noticed our strength and added more. So we tell people that Pradip has already won the election."

Indeed, Parag Patel, a second-generation Gujarati lawyer, is running for Edison City Council on the Democratic ticket, an announcement made after Pradip had thrown his hat in. Patel had tried to get involved in politics the year before, and the party never called him back. This year is different, as the Democrats needed viable candidates to fill their slate for council positions. So the party was sure to call Patel this year.

At Pradip's makeshift headquarters, his daughters stop by around 4:00 P.M., both on their way to night classes.

"Dad, I need you to buy an ad for the Diwali program," says Toral. She's doing a dance at NYU's celebration of the holiday. "Oh and do you know any videographers we can hire for it?"

Pradip looks through his tattered address book, finds a card, and hands it to her. "Try this," he says. "And go to my office and ask them for an old ad. Just reprint that."

They each hug him before they leave. "Good luck," they call out.

Pradip is about to call EBC radio, a station in Edison devoted to Indian American programming. He turns to Jesel and asks, "So what should I say?"

"Lay it on thick about bias incidents after September 11. And just tell them what you have been saying all along."

The Republicans count on getting most of their votes between 6:00 and 8:00 P.M., after the workday ends. Pradip decides to head over to J. P. Stevens High School to see how the turnout looks. There, he encounters an Indian woman working as a Democratic challenger who charges that one of Pradip's supporters verbally threatened her for not accepting votes from two residents, who happen to be Republican. A brief argument ensues, and Pradip's temper starts to show hints of flaring. Quickly, his entourage ushers him out, leaving the disputed votes in their own Republican challenger's hands.

Together, they drive to Victorian Plaza; the strip mall, lit in neon, looks anything but Victorian. By this time, Jesel has called Pradip on his cell phone to tell him it's not looking good. Back at the house, the desi volunteers stop their work, cramming into an upstairs room with a television to view the returns. They cheer when Parag Patel and Upendra Chivukula win. They debate ordering out from a diner or an Indian restaurant for dinner. They decide to wait for Pradip to decide.

At the headquarters, Pradip and his friends try to look busy. They eat sandwiches, munch on chips, drink canned sodas. A woman with gray curly hair takes returns over the phone as

Pradip's running mate, Tina, her husband, sheriff candidate Tom Owen, and other party brass hear the results. They crack jokes and smoke cigarettes, and the Indians smile politely but say little. It is clear they don't quite belong yet.

The same can be said for the Republicans in Middlesex County. As it has every year, it doesn't look good for any of the GOP candidates. Occasionally, Pradip's friends go outside to smoke their own cigarettes or talk in their native language. Until this visit, they had been filled with hope, the hope that every underdog clings to.

When the word comes in that Schundler has accepted defeat, Pradip's friends ask him where he wants to be when he accepts his own: the insurance office or back at the makeshift campaign headquarters.

"Let's go home," he says.

Home.

The house-turned-office falls silent as Pradip walks in. How to greet a loser? Then slowly the group of hungry, waiting men starts to clap and cheer. Pradip is quiet, for even the candidate expecting defeat remains stung by it.

But as he hears the applause and gazes out onto the crowd, the bitterness of loss temporarily subsides. For here, at home, he feels victorious.

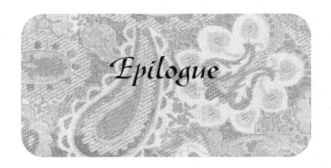

Epilogue

In the late nineteenth century, tourists descended upon Edison to gawk at its Christmas lights displays and witness for themselves the place where "tomorrow was born," as township officials often boast. As Edison entered the twenty-first century, two of every ten people were of Indian origin. And 55,000 Indians were counted by the census in Middlesex County alone—one-third of all the Indians who live in New Jersey. Many, such as Pradip and Nandini Kothari, call it home. Some, such as Sankumani and Shravani Sarma, are starting to like the sound of that. And others, such as Harish Patel, don't know if they ever will.

Despite a sluggish economy and a slowdown in immigration after the events of September 11, America continues to beckon. And as the explosion in central New Jersey's Indian population shows, it is the suburb—with all its promise—that lures. In so many ways, central Jersey reflects the quintessential suburban towns that dot the U.S. landscape, with mini-malls and gas stations and monster movie theaters. Yet supermarkets now carry okra and cardamom, movie theaters roll Bollywood flicks, and senior centers feature meditation. Indeed, immigration has altered the American suburb, and the suburb, in turn, has altered the immigrant. Once again, Edison might be the community that has shown us the future.

Here, Pradip Kothari achieved economic equality with his neighbors and went on to wage a quest for political parity. Toral Kothari spent high school dances grooving to Top 40 but twirled on autumn weekend nights to garba. Whiz kids Sankumani and Shravani Sarma left a rapidly Americanizing India, only to find a rapidly Indianizing suburbia. In an act of suburban disobedience, Kapila Patel never learned to drive, paying a man a dollar a day to take her to her livelihood until she lost her job. Kajal Patel punched codes into a supermarket cash register, all the while hoping the computer code she studied in college might ultimately make her journey less arduous than her parents'.

As of this writing, Harish still worked as a security guard but continued to look for a better job. Kapila remained unemployed. Kajal transferred to Rutgers University and expected to graduate with a major in economics and a minor in psychology in December 2003. Zankhana, Bittu, and Simran still live in Rochester but visit Edison every few months so Simran and her new little brother, Sahil-Deep, can visit their grandparents and practice their Gujarati. Harish says he still has dreams of retiring in India, once Kajal is settled and his debts are paid.

In the fall of 2002, the Sarmas received their green cards, shortly after they bought a home in Marlboro, New Jersey. In October 2002, Shravani gave birth to a second baby boy, Abhijat. Sanku started a traveling musicians' group to perform ghazals and other classical Indian music. Siku started first grade; he speaks fluent Assamese and English. His grandparents visited for six months when his little brother was born. In those months, neither child needed day care.

After his loss, Pradip Kothari gave up running Navratri to devote more time to his business and local politics. With Pradip's diminished involvement, his family stopped feeling obligated to attend the festival every weekend. Nandini continued working at four hospitals, adding hours to her schedule. Payal, a senior at Kean, started to look for jobs in health-care consulting. And Toral, a sophomore at NYU, prepared to study abroad in London. The festival went on, of course, drawing thousands of Indians synchronizing with the familiar sounds and steps. In central New Jersey, the search for home continued.

Notes

INTRODUCTION

Most of the data in this chapter cite the source directly. All population data are taken from the U.S. Census. Characterizations of historic Edison and Woodbridge came from the local chambers of commerce and interviews with David Sheehan, Edison's amateur historian. The Center for Immigration provided data in two abstracts. Immigration history was liberally summarized from years of reporting on the subject and interviews with numerous experts.

PROLOGUE: A NEW YEAR

Most of this chapter is based on conversations and actions I witnessed, as well as interviews I conducted. I attended four of the five Navratri weekends held in Edison in 2000. I also accompanied the Sarmas to Durga Puja on October 7, 2000. Additional material was taken from:

Canonie, Deborah. "Navratri Draws 4,000." *Home News Tribune,* Oct. 13, 1996.

Gallotto, Anthony A. "Curfew Battle Clouds Festival." *Star-Ledger,* Oct. 13, 1997.

Goodnough, Abby. "Indian Celebration Draws Happy Throngs, and Complaints." *New York Times,* Oct. 1, 1995, sec. 13NJ.

Kauffman, Matthew. "Bradlees Gets out of Court; Chain Leaves Chapter 11, but Faces Powerful Rivals." *Hartford Courant,* Feb. 4, 1999.

Lefkowitz, Melanie. "Worries about Security at SJU." *Newsday,* May 29, 2001.

Reidy, Chris. "Bradlees Reports Loss for Period." *Boston Globe,* Nov. 16, 2000.

CHAPTER 1. DEPORTED FROM HOME

This chapter is based on numerous interviews with and observations of the Kothari family. On April 25 and 26, 2001, I interviewed

Ramanlal and Sumati Kothari in their home in Baroda. Statistics were culled from the U.S. Census and an article from *American Demographics* magazine, formally cited below. Additional material was taken from:

Associated Press. "Civil Rights Charges Dropped in Beating of Asian-Indian Physician." June 18, 1993.

———. "Man Acquitted in Assault on Indian Doctor." May 30, 1993.

Burney, Melanie. "Trio Acquitted in Hudson Beating Case." Associated Press, Feb. 10, 1993.

Burns, Frances Ann. "Asian Indians Organizing for Political Clout." United Press International, Aug. 12, 1989.

Chen, David. "Asian Middle Class Alters a Rural Enclave." *New York Times,* Dec. 27, 1999.

"Coping with Cleveland Winters." About.com travel guide to Cleveland.

Daniels, Lee A. "City Apartment Hunt: Tale of Sore Feet and Sad Luck." *New York Times,* June 20, 1981.

Deshpande, Shubada. "Hilltop Nagar." *Little India*, Sept. 1999

Hanley, Robert. "In Edison, a Crossroads of Diversity." *New York Times,* Apr. 17, 1991.

James, George. "Jersey Murder Trial Is Bias Issue for Indians." *New York Times,* Mar. 14, 1989.

Kamen, Al. "After Immigration, an Unexpected Fear; New Jersey's Indian Community Is Terrorized by Racial Violence." *Washington Post,* Nov. 16, 1992.

Krugman, Paul. *Peddling Prosperity: Economic Sense and Nonsense in the Age of Diminished Expectations.* New York: W. W. Norton, 1994.

Kunkle, Frederick. "Key Figure Sentenced in Attacks on Indians." *Bergen Record,* Feb. 9, 1991.

Levitt, David M. "Edison Housing Favors Affluent." *News Tribune,* Sept. 5, 1986.

———. "In Edison, a New Image on Route 1." *News Tribune,* Nov. 2, 1986.

Melwani, Lavina. "The Gujaratis." *Little India*, Feb. 2002.

Mogelonsky, Marcia. "Asian-Indian Americans." *American Demographics,* August 1995.

Oser, Alan. "About Real Estate: Costs and Manhattan Rental Construction." *New York Times,* Sept. 26, 1980.

Peterson, Iver. "County by County, a Fight against Bias." *New York Times,* Jan. 5, 1993.

Walt, Vivienne. "A New Racism Gets Violent in New Jersey." *Newsday,* Apr. 6, 1988.

CHAPTER 2. THE PATELS' JOURNEY

This chapter is based on numerous interviews with and observations of the Patel family. On April 25, 2001, I visited their old home in Baroda, as well as the Bank of Baroda, where Harish Patel once worked. Additional material, much of it tracked down by research assistant Beth Kressel, was taken from:

"Analysts Are Divided over Next Move." *Star-Ledger,* May 17, 1987.
Associated Press. "Economic Signs Point to Inflation Increase." May 17, 1987.
———. "Housing Construction Plunges 11% amid Concerns of Rising Mortgages." Mar. 19, 1985.
———. "Industrials Drop 15 in Volatile Session." May 11, 1987.
———. "Industrials Soar 21.42 Percent as Gold Prices Rocket." Mar. 19, 1985.
Baehr, Guy T. "Seven States Ready to Hike Gasoline Tax." *Star-Ledger,* May 13, 1987.
Clark, Lindley H., Jr., and Alfred L. Malabre Jr. "Productivity Indicates Sluggish Economy." *Wall Street Journal,* July 6, 1990.
"Confidence Hurt." *Star-Ledger,* Mar. 20, 1985.
"Employee Aid Packages Advance." *Star-Ledger,* Dec. 2, 1988.
Herman, Tom. "Lower Interest Rates Will Aid Economy, Help Avert Recession, but Growth Will Be Very Weak, Says Survey of 40 Economists." *Wall Street Journal,* July 5, 1990.
Osborne, Judith. "AT&T to Trim 16,000; 'Minimal' in the State." *Star-Ledger,* Dec. 2, 1988.
"State Jobless Claims Rose in June 23 Week." *Wall Street Journal*, July 6, 1990.
Tanner, James. "Oil Prices Skid on Concerns about Output." *Wall Street Journal*, Oct. 3, 1988.

CHAPTER 3. A GOLD-PAVED ENTRY

This chapter is based on numerous interviews with and observations of the Sarma family. On April 18, 2001, I interviewed Shravani's parents in Guwahati, India, and attended her cousin's marriage. On April 28, I visited the Sarmas' old home in the Godrej colony in the Vikroli section of Bombay and interviewed their family friends and neighbors. Some of the material for this chapter originally appeared in *Newsday* in July 2001, in a series I wrote entitled "The New India." Suketu Mehta, a writer in New York, provided expertise and context on Bombay. Additional material was taken from:

Saxenian, AnnaLee. *Silicon Valley's New Immigrant Entrepreneurs.* San Francisco: Public Policy Institute of California, 1999.

CHAPTER 4. EXERCISING RIGHTS

This chapter is based on interviews with and observations of the Patel family.

CHAPTER 5. WANTING MORE

This chapter is based on numerous interviews with and observations of the Kothari family. Additional material is taken from:

Prashad, Vijay. *The Karma of Brown Folk.* Minneapolis: University of Minnesota Press, 2000.
Purewal, Sukhjit. "S. Asian Students Fest in San Francisco." India Abroad News Service, Jan. 13, 2001.
Srivastava, Deepali. "From 'Little India' to Washington." MSNBC.com, Mar. 16, 2000.

CHAPTER 6. SHAKY GROUND

This chapter is based on numerous interviews with and observations of the Sarma family.

Additional material is taken from:

Healy, Beth. "Lucent Group Looks Within for Ideas to Take Market." *Boston Globe,* Feb. 28, 2000.
Robinson, Sara. "High-Tech Workers Are Trapped in Limbo by I.N.S." *New York Times,* Feb. 29, 2000.
Saxenian, AnnaLee. *Silicon Valley's New Immigrant Entrepreneurs.* San Francisco: Public Policy Institute of California, 1999.

CHAPTER 7. DESTRUCTIVE TIMES

This chapter is based on numerous interviews with and observations of the Patel family.

CHAPTER 8. STANDING ROOM ONLY

This chapter is based on numerous interviews with and observations of the Kothari family. Brian Selander provided much insight on Middlesex County politics and history. Portions are also taken from a story I wrote for Rediff.com. Research assistant Beth Kressel helped run the population data. Statistics were derived from the U.S. Census and various New Jersey School Report Cards. Additional material is taken from:

Prashad, Vijay. *The Karma of Brown Folk.* Minneapolis: University of Minnesota Press, 2000.
Purewal, Sukhjit. "S. Asian Students Fest in San Francisco." India Abroad News Service, Jan. 13, 2001.
Srivastava, Deepali. "From 'Little India' to Washington." MSNBC.com, Mar. 16, 2000.

CHAPTER 9. DOWNTURNS

This chapter is based on numerous interviews with and observations of the Sarma family. Additional material is taken from:

Johnson, Carrie. "High-Tech Visa Approvals Down from Last Year." *Washington Post,* Mar. 21, 2001.
Lubman, Sarah. "Demand Slows for Foreign Workers." *San Jose Mercury News,* Mar. 21, 2001.

CHAPTER 10. UNDER A MANGO TREE

This chapter is based on numerous interviews with and observations of the Patel family. On April 25, 2001, I toured Baroda with the Patels' family friend Kemas Wadia. Interviews were conducted with friends, family, and former colleagues where noted. Suketu Mehta provided information on Bollywood.

CHAPTER 11. MEETING ELEPHANTS

This chapter is based on numerous interviews with and observations of the Kothari family. I thank Melanie Cooper-Cortese and Iris Milstein for their helpful comments on their hometown of South Plainfield. Additional material is taken from:

Rajan, Sujeet. "Primary Colors." *Indian Express,* June 22, 2001.
Walsh, Diane. "The Real Freeholder Candidates Step Up." *Star-Ledger,* Aug. 10, 2001.

CHAPTER 12. FAREWELLS

This chapter is based on numerous interviews with and observations of the Sarma family.

CHAPTER 13. THE FESTIVAL FAMILY

This chapter is based on numerous interviews with and observations of the Kothari family.

Additional material is taken from:

Joshi, Monika. "Indians Shed Fear, Don Garba Shoes for Navratri." *India Abroad*, Nov. 2, 2001.

CHAPTER 14. CLASSIFIED

This chapter is based on numerous interviews with and observations of the Patel family.

CHAPTER 15. THE VICTOR

This chapter is based on numerous interviews with and observations of the Kothari family. I spent Election Day with Pradip Kothari and his volunteer crew.

Selected Bibliography

Duany, Andres, Elizabeth Plater-Zyberk, and Jeff Speck. *Suburban Nation: The Rise of Sprawl and the Decline of the American Dream.* New York: North Point Press, 2000.

Karasik, Gary, and Anna M. Aschkenes. *Middlesex County: Crossroads of History.* Sun Valley, Calif.: American Historical Press, 1999.

Maira, Sunaina Marr. *Desis in the House: Indian American Youth Culture in New York City.* Philadelphia: Temple University Press, 2002.

Prashad, Vijay. *The Karma of Brown Folk.* Minneapolis: University of Minnesota Press, 2000.

Saxenian, AnnaLee. *Silicon Valley's New Immigrant Entrepreneurs.* San Francisco: Public Policy Institute of California, 1999.

Sheehan, David. *Welcome to Edison: An Enlightened Community.* Edison: Edison Township Historical Society, 1991.

About the Author

S. Mitra Kalita is a staff writer for the *Washington Post* covering education. She has received numerous journalism awards, and previously worked for *Newsday* and the Associated Press. The daughter of immigrants from the Indian state of Assam, Mitra has lived in Washington, New York City, Long Island, Puerto Rico, and the suburbs of New Jersey. She has written extensively about immigration and the South Asian diaspora and serves as president of the South Asian Journalists Association. This is her first book.